AF583583

First published in 2014 by Caralee Caldwell

PHOTOGRAPHY & FOOD STYLING

Jo Anderson

www.theluminouskitchen.com.au

ALL RECIPES

Caralee Caldwell

FOOD PREPARATION

Caralee Caldwell & Jo Anderson

ART DIRECTION/PRODUCTION

Caralee Caldwell

DESIGN

Ian Gay & Belinda Greenwood,
Shac Communications

Printed in China by Toppan Leefung Printing Limited

ISBN 978-0-9941691-0-5

www.realfoodpledge.com

Strategies for cutting out processed food, getting off the diet roller coaster and living a real food lifestyle.

40+ GLUTEN, DAIRY & SUGAR FREE RECIPES

CARALEE CALDWELL

CONTENTS

PART ONE

PART TWO – RECIPES

FOREWORD

BY LUKE HINES

Healthy food can be tasty food! This is a line that I said half way through the adventure that was My Kitchen Rules. It has stuck strong with me all the way from that Kitchen Headquarters to writing this foreword today for the inspiring and talented Caralee. This belief that healthy food is in fact tasty is what led me to meet this inspiring author. I met Caralee in Brisbane during a tour I was doing called The Paleo Way. In a room full of thousands of people, something just stood out. When you meet certain people, you can see a sparkle in their eye that speaks volumes about their passion, integrity and commitment to fighting the good fight. That is why I am so honoured and humbled to be writing this piece today, as I am writing it for someone who not only knows their stuff, but has a true love for it inside them that is evident in this stunning book.

Through my mission statement—train hard, eat clean and feel good—my life is all about educating people on training functionally, eating as clean as you can sustainably, and keeping a balanced and healthy headspace for a positive lifestyle. And I believe it can be simple. Training has been my background for a long time, however the overall "Clean Living" message that I now love to promote was launched by my stint on the 2013 series of *My Kitchen Rules*. *My Kitchen Rules* gave me a platform to show Australia how to cook nutritious, yet delicious, creations in their own homes. I set out to prove that you don't need to be a full-time chef to make amazing meals that contribute towards optimal health. Post *My Kitchen Rules,* I noticed an encouraging eagerness of the public to continue learning about my clean living lifestyle. This led to the release of my Clean Living Cook book series, which includes training plans and mouth-watering, paleo-style recipes.

REAL FOOD PLEDGE IS RELATABLE, INFORMATIVE AND HONEST.

I don't believe that eating well should be complicated, and Caralee encapsulates this in *Real Food Pledge* by taking it back to basics with information to arm readers with knowledge to make their own positive food choices. Much of the modern world that we live in is over-stimulated and over-complicated, but after reading this book it is hoped you will realise that at least the food part of your lifestyle doesn't need to be this way. A major struggle in the modern world with regards to our food choices is dissecting the abundance of information and varieties that are available. A main benefit of reading this book is the education that it provides you with to make your own food choices that will improve you. You will learn that rather than being a diet to follow, pledging to eat real food is a lifestyle that leads people towards optimal health and well-being. A lifestyle means something you can sustain for you and your loved ones, long term, to live your best life.

You will learn as you read this book, and as I try to show people myself, you do not miss out on flavour, meals or occasions when you follow a real food lifestyle. From pancakes for breakfast to cheesecake for dessert, it is likely that all of your favourite meals can be made using real food so that you never leave your taste palate unsatisfied. There are so many tasty flavours that can be found in natural, real food sourced and eaten in its purest form. Both of my books, and now Caralee's *Real Food Pledge* book, show you just some of the wonderful flavour combinations that are available without compromising on quality or your health. The delicious recipes demonstrate that you can make these nutritious creations in your own kitchen and around your already busy lifestyle.

Real Food Pledge is a prime example of an everyday person who has personally experienced the positive benefits of switching to a real food lifestyle, and wants to spread the eat clean message to benefit the lives of others too. Caralee recounts her personal story about switching from being addicted to processed food and being on a diet roller coaster to a real food lifestyle and having a healthier well-being. *Real Food Pledge* is relatable, informative and honest.

This is the type of book that will be a staple in your home, not just for a week, but for a lifetime. Her easy to follow, affordable recipes will leave even the toughest judge speechless, with the flavours speaking for themselves. Just like Caralee, make a real food pledge and change your life for the better, today.

trainerluke.com

I'm done with COMPLICATED EATING KISS*

Why does eating always have to seem so complicated? There are so many dos and don'ts! It actually doesn't need to be hard, and in this book we are going to get back to the basics and learn to love real food again.

Real food is meant to be enjoyed, savoured and loved. You should never feel guilty or eat something that you don't enjoy. You should actually want to eat foods that are good for you, and it shouldn't require complicated calculations, apps, point counting or measurements to figure out what you should and shouldn't eat.

This book arms you with how to focus on real, whole foods (the types of foods that our great-grandparents would have eaten) and how to make real food delicious without feeling like the nutrition and diet police are out to get us every time we open our mouths.

In this book you will learn why you should cut processed food from your life, how to identify real food from fake food, how to navigate the modern world of food, and what a real food lifestyle looks like. This is an account of my personal journey from a modern day processed food lifestyle to a real food lifestyle. This is not a diet book! I am not a dietitian, nutritionist or doctor. I am actually a lawyer, so naturally I love to give advice and argue a point! I am passionate about how real food has positively changed my life and made me a happier, healthier person. I love to share the good news through my recipes, blog and now this book.

[*KEEP IT SIMPLE, STUPID!]

If you're in a place where you want to make some changes, get off the diet roller coaster, feel vibrant and healthy, and look fantastic, but you are unsure of how to go about it, I am so glad you're here! ◆

MY STORY

In August 2013, I gave up processed food. I cut it out of my life. I stopped the diet roller coaster and I became a happier, healthier, and stronger person. I was sick and tired of feeling like rubbish, starting the Monday diet that would peter out by Thursday, then to only start again on Monday. I wanted to feel good all the time, so I successfully quit processed food – permanently. And you know what... I have never felt better.

Over time I have consulted experts, read countless books, and continued to research, read and educate myself on the subject of food. At the end of this book is a list of resources if you would like to read and learn more. I tried to cut out processed food on numerous occasions without success, but then I cracked the code and have now successfully changed to a real food lifestyle. I will never look back. My mother and my grandmother got on board. They too cut out processed food. We all committed to improving our food choices and our lives. It didn't stop there. My husband also got rid of processed food once he saw the difference that it made to me. The health benefits and the results were incredible! My husband dropped 10kg effortlessly, and he hasn't looked back.

I have been so inspired by my life change and the life changes of the people around me, no matter their age or gender. I want to share with you my experience of what has worked, so that you too can make the leap to a healthier life.

We have all grown up with certain ideas about food, about what is healthy and what is not. We have been lied to, marketed to and sold to. We don't even know what healthy, real foods are anymore! Many of us have been on low fat, highly processed, low calorie diets for years or even decades, and we all seem to be fatter, sicker and unhappier than ever. We are digging our own graves with our knives and forks! ◆

I HAVE NEVER FELT BETTER

WHAT WILL YOU LEARN?

This book will show you how to get rid of fake, processed food from your life, how to replace it with real food so that you feel energized, improve your health, and maybe even lose weight. It's a step-by-step guide full of tips and techniques that helped me eliminate processed food for good.

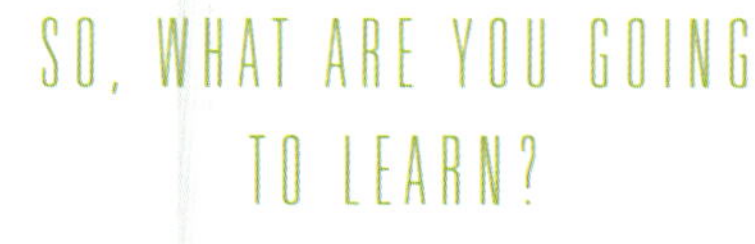

1 How to identify what addiction to processed food looks like.

2 Why the food you are eating keeps you craving more.

3

How to tackle your processed food addiction.

4

How to recognise foods to avoid and foods to enjoy.

5

How to navigate the modern, processed-food world that we live in.

6

How to cook simple but tasty recipes for everyday real-food meals including breakfast, lunch, dinner and treats.

my addiction TO PROCESSED FOOD

[AND BEING A SERIAL DIETER]

I never thought that I had an addiction. I have never smoked cigarettes or needed alcohol. In my mind, I was fortunate that I didn't suffer from any addictions. However, I never realised that the very reason I could not resist a bread roll on the table, say no to a dessert, or was constantly reaching for another handful of chips and thinking about what dinner might be (while I was still eating lunch) was because...

I had an addiction to processed food! I was even addicted to what I thought was healthy – low fat foods, health bars, health shakes and low fat frozen meals.

As a child I ate fairly well without a lot of processed foods. We never had muesli bars or cookies. However, as I became a teenager in the 90's, processed foods started to take hold. For lunch I would eat an entire can of spaghetti with buttery toast. I could not wait for my next lolly fix, and I was compelled to eat sweets after my carb-loaded processed dinner each night.

I then hit adulthood and was subjected to my first diet when I was nineteen years old. It was a program where I was assigned my own supportive consultant and ate pre-prepared packet food. I remember the first day of the diet. I came home with my food, opened the packet, and cried because the meal looked so tiny. I told myself it would be ok and that I could still drink diet soft drinks! I used to consume obscene amounts, because I thought that diet soft drinks would not contribute to my weight issues. I now know differently.

I needed to check in each week to be weighed as well as collect my food for the next week. When you are a constant dieter, there is a method to weigh ins. Everyone has a unique method. Mine was regimented; I would ensure that I got an appointment early in the day. I wouldn't eat breakfast or drink anything, and I would make sure I was wearing my lightest clothes possible. I would go to the bathroom right before I left the house and then again when I got to the consultation just to make sure that I was not one ounce heavier than I needed to be! Then I was ready to jump on the scale. Oh wait, I needed to take off my shoes and jewellery. Ok, now I was ready to weigh in! How completely ridiculous! However, after I had been starving for a week on low fat, pre-packaged, processed foods, I did not want to be disappointed by the amount of weight I had lost.

I lost 12kg on my first diet through eating a highly processed, calorie restricted diet of microwave meals. It was a success. I lost weight, and that was the purpose, right? Wrong! That diet was the beginning of more than thirteen years of calorie controlled, highly processed and constant diets, struggles with my weight, and obsessive behaviour regarding my relationship with food and the bathroom scales.

Like a lot of people, I have tried them all. I was a serial dieter. I counted points, went to weigh ins, had consultants, tried pre-prepared, low carb and no carb meals, counted calories, experimented with drops, pills, shakes and potions. Each time I tried a new diet, I would have a renewed hope for a magical result.

My relationship with food had two phases, the first one being very restrictive and bordering on starvation, or the opposite – binge eating. The next was feeling guilty about bingeing only to go back on a starvation diet… again. I was on a diet roller coaster that I could not get off, and I didn't know why.

Because of this reactionary eating, I developed mood disorders and sleep problems, and I could not control my weight. I also had gut problems, tummy aches, hot and cold sweats, and would spend long periods of times in the bathroom, thinking that this was completely normal. ◆

What changed MY LIFE?

Four years ago I spent three weeks in Thailand on a family holiday. We made the rule that while we were there we would only eat local food. We made it clear to the children that we would not allow pizza, French fries, breads or burgers – only Thai food. We ate Thai food for breakfast, lunch and dinner, and I felt fantastic!

We were eating lots of fresh vegetables, fruits and meats. We were not eating any bread, wheat, dairy or refined sugar. When I returned from my holiday, I thought that I would continue that at home for a four-week period as a "diet" since I wanted to lose weight. I lost five kilos in four weeks, while eating as many fruits, vegetables and meat as I wanted. I truly felt amazing.

The problem was, I still had a "diet" mentality. I was always on a diet to lose weight, and while this one was a healthy one compared to my past processed versions, it was still a temporary diet. As usual, I could not wait for four weeks to pass so I could binge on my favourite foods – sushi, yum cha, buttery toast and fat reduced desserts. Of course, I went back to my normal eating and quickly found the five kilos I had lost. I didn't feel good; I continued my quest for a miracle diet to lose weight. I could not kick my addiction, and I continued to hunt for quick fixes. ◆

WHY DID I FINALLY TAKE A Real Food Pledge?

1

I was so sick and tired of being on the diet roller coaster.

I was a serial dieter and I had had enough! I knew there must be a better way to live. I did not want to be on and off diets for the rest of my life. I hated it, and sometimes I hated myself.

2

I had zero will power.

If someone put a bread roll and butter, a piece of cake, or a plate of crackers in front of me, I would just wolf it down! Once I got a taste, I couldn't control myself. I have learned that it was not my fault. These processed products are designed for you to lose control.

I had many digestive issues.

From the time I was very small, I can remember spending long periods of time in the bathroom. I would often experience hot and cold flushes and tummy aches, I thought it was normal to feel gassy or bloated and be constipated, or have diarrhoea. Processed foods were the cause of all of these symptoms and I wanted a happy tummy!

4

I wanted to lose and easily maintain my weight.

I'd put on weight (7kg) from having a child and my constant diet and binge lifestyle didn't help. I really wanted to shift the weight and also maintain weight loss with little effort.

5

I wanted to feel better on the inside and out.

I was sick of beating myself up and hating myself because of the poor choices that I was making in regards to food. If I honoured myself more by feeding my body with quality food, then I would be able to love myself more easily.

6

I wanted to live longer.

I wanted to increase my chances of living a long, happy and healthy life. The more I learned, the more I realised that cutting out processed food was so much more than just about losing weight. There are so many advantages, and the big-ticket item is a long and healthy life. Who wants to be only 60 years old or younger, suffering from diabetes, heart disease and arthritis just to name a few? Not me!

Processed Foods
THE GOOD, THE BAD, & THE DOWNRIGHT UGLY

You might be wondering – do I need to cut processed food out and make a real food pledge?

I don't know you or your circumstances, so I can't answer that question for you. This book is about my story and sharing information I learned, and amazing real food recipes, with you. I want to show you how easy it is to live a real food lifestyle. It is up to you whether you think a real food lifestyle is right for you and your personal circumstances.

What I will say to you is that there is no harm in trying this out for 28 days to see if it helps you feel and look better. If any of the following on the next page describe you, you have nothing to lose and everything to gain by taking your own real food pledge for 28 days. ☞

Have an unhappy tummy?

Get gassy and bloated?

Not sleep well?

Have an energy slump in the afternoon?

Lack energy in general?

Always hunt for something sweet after dinner or in the afternoon?

Often feel unclear and have a foggy brain?

Always think about when you are going to eat next?

Look in the mirror and do the self-loathe thing?

Obsess with your weight and always think about going on a diet?

Always go on and off diets?

Binge eat uncontrollably?

I answered "yes" to all of the above and had a sneaking suspicion that manufactured, fake food was not helping. If you can relate too, then you should consider giving it a go. I can guarantee that having a real food lifestyle has changed my life in so many positive ways.

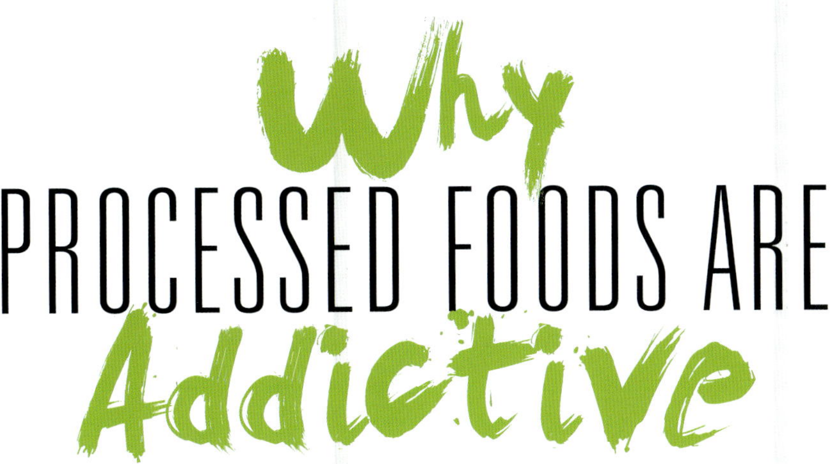

Why PROCESSED FOODS ARE Addictive

We are led to believe there are no good or bad foods – that it's all a matter of balance. You have heard sayings like "moderation is key" and "to have a balanced diet". If we were talking about anything else that is addictive like cocaine or cigarettes, we wouldn't talk about moderation or balance.

New discoveries in science prove that industrially processed and sugar, fat and salt-laden foods (food that is made in a plant, rather than grown on a plant, as Michael Pollan would say) are addictive. The good news about this is that it is not your fault that you cannot stop. The bad news is that you are actually addicted to processed foods, and that is why you cannot stop.

Imagine a metre high pile of chopped carrots, a huge T-bone steak or a giant bowl of apple slices. Do you know anyone who would binge on carrots, steak or apples? Now imagine a mountain of salty potato chips, a whole bag of cookies or a huge tub of ice cream. Ahhh, yes I can see you picturing it now! It is really easy to imagine inhaling a mountain of salty potato chips or devouring a bag of cookies. Carrots and apples are not addictive, but cookies, chips or soda absolutely can be. ☞

[IF IT IS ADDICTIVE AND CAN KILL YOU AFTER YEARS OF USE, WE ARE WARNED TO STAY AWAY FROM IT.]

It is very hard, if not impossible, to just say "no" to something that you have an addiction to. You may be like I was and deny that you have an addiction. But if you find it hard to give up the processed foods in your fridge and cupboards, I dare say that you have a problem, just as I did.

Michael Moss, an investigative reporter and the author of Salt Sugar Fat, dissects the $1 trillion processed food industry and tells how concerted and targeted the effort is by food companies to hit the magical formulation. He was surprised to learn how food inventors and scientists spend a huge amount of money and time formulating the perfect amount of sugar, salt and fat that will send us over the moon and send products flying off the shelves.

> IT IS TIME TO TAKE CONTROL AND SAY NO MORE TO BEING MARKETED TO BY THESE LARGE FOOD MANUFACTURERS AS I HAVE DONE.

Why would you want to be sucked in to buying and eating products that are designed to hook you by their addictive, carefully selected ingredients? Furthermore, these products are making us overweight and sick! It is time to take control and say no to being marketed to by these large food manufacturers as I have done.

The advantage of cutting out processed foods (apart from weight loss and being a healthier you) is the huge world of wonderful food that will open up to you. You will not miss out on amazing flavours, textures and taste sensations. In fact, you might be surprised to learn that it is quite the opposite. I will share with you my amazing real food recipes and ingredients that will have your taste buds zinging, beginning at page 54.

When you are not shoving processed rubbish into your mouth, you are giving yourself the opportunity to explore healthier options that will tantalise your taste buds. I can reassure you that I never miss out on beautiful treats, desserts and breads. Yes it is true, you can enjoy all of these foods even when you ONLY eat real food. It is quite amazing and exciting. ◆

smile

ARE YOU

It is not easy to kick addictions. That is a fact! You may still be in denial that you have an addiction to processed food. Just remember, if you find it hard to stop, that is because it is. It is hard. You may hit a wall and feel like rubbish at first. But I promise once you have felt how amazing your body is meant to feel, you will not want to go back. When you think about it, our bodies are NOT meant to eat processed food; our bodies are designed to eat natural food.

When you first give up processed foods, you may feel bad for a few days. It is more challenging for some people than others. Just think, if you feel bad coming off the processed foods, how are they actually affecting your body?

Just so that you are prepared, you may experience the following in the first 5 to 10 days:

- A mild headache, on and off, that can last for a couple of days
- Low energy and feeling tired
- Mood swings and feeling cranky

It is not your fault that you are addicted to processed food; the food manufacturers have got you right where they want you. Think about it. If you are addicted to their foods, what will you do? Bingo! You will keep buying their foods. ◆

> IT IS NOT YOUR FAULT THAT YOU ARE ADDICTED TO PROCESSED FOOD.

A REAL LOOK AT PROCESSED FOODS

The undercover culprits

Fried foods, chocolate, cakes, fast foods and pizza might come to mind when you think about processed foods, but don't be fooled. There is a huge range of food that is marketed to us as being "healthy". However, that is far from the truth.

Your local supermarket and even health food store shelves are lined with products that claim to be balanced, healthy, low fat, low GI and super foods. There are products such as salad dressings, breads, milks, yoghurt, crackers, low fat products and cereals, just to name a few, that are not as healthy as they seem at first blush. I would be so bold as to say that if it is in a package, it has a probable chance of being what I would class as a "fake" food.

When products are genetically modified, pasteurised, refined, dehydrated, canned, concentrated, extracted, or put through any other industrial process, the food is stripped of all its naturally present flavour, fibre, phytonutrients, and most of the vitamins and minerals too. The manufacturers then add all sorts of sugars, industrial oils, fake fibre, preservatives, chemicals and synthetic nutrients.

Why do manufacturers do this? It sounds crazy that manufacturers would go through all this effort to transform real food into fake food. They do not care about your health. If they can make products cheaper that last longer, taste sweeter or saltier and make your body crave more, they make more money. Simple!

When you eat empty, processed foods that lack the naturally present fibre and nutrients of real foods, you'll find yourself "starving" again within an hour or so, and you will be hunting for your next fix. Before I gave up processed foods, I would eat breakfast but by 10am, I was on the hunt for something else to eat.

When you are eating a diet of processed foods, I am not just talking about what you think would be classified as "junk" foods. This also includes foods that are marketed as low carb, low fat, low GI, healthy products. With these products, you are actually loading up on an exorbitant number of empty calories. Your body is simply not getting the essential nutrients it needs to fire up its metabolic processes. Your appetite switch never really turns off. Pretty soon, you're ravenous, and it's not real nutrient dense food that your body wants. Instead, it craves the empty, processed food you're addicted to.

ANOTHER SNACK ANYONE?

The price you ultimately pay for your addiction and for the convenience is a high one. I know that this sounds dramatic, but it is true. The price of your addiction could shorten your life by decades. And, if it doesn't shorten your life, your quality of life is decreased because as you get older, you and your doctor will know each other more than you would like!

These addictive, processed food products leave you forever battling with your weight, experiencing wild mood swings and brain fog, feeling completely wiped of energy, and on top of all that, feeling guilty for each and every little morsel you eat.

Does that sound familiar to you? That is how it was for me.

Are you like I used to be – starting another diet on Monday or planning on being "good" next month? STOP!

Put an end to this craziness forever by choosing a real food lifestyle. The bonus is that you will enjoy a longer, healthier and happier life.

The only way you can do that is by fully cutting out processed, fake food forever.

PUT AN END TO THIS CRAZINESS FOREVER BY CHOOSING A REAL FOOD LIFESTYLE.

If you eat it, you crave more. It has to be gone for the addictive behaviour to change.

Bear with me. Don't be stressed. We can fix this problem.

I am going to share with you how I got rid of processed food, got my health back on track and my weight under control.

Not only did I do it, but so did my mother who is in her 50's, my grandmother who is in her late 70's, and my husband, as well as hundreds of others who follow my blog.

We are different ages and genders, and we all did it. You can too! ☞

The Sour ON PROCESSED FOODS

We can all agree that processed or "junk" food is not good for us, and that we will not be healthier if we consume lots of factory-made food loaded with chemicals. There is no argument about that, but what is processed food, and why is it so bad?

Processed food is any form of food that has been through a process and has had ingredients added or nutrients taken out. Basically, if you cannot make it in your own kitchen, it is probably processed. The foods that contain refined sugar, grains, soy, processed dairy and industrial oils should be avoided. Here is why...

Refined Sugar

Refined sugar comes in many forms and whether it is white, brown, raw, corn syrup, glucose or cane sugar, just to name a few, it has generally been processed through extreme chemical purification, heat treatments, and bleaching.

[REFINED SUGARS ARE NUTRIENT-VOID, CALORIE DENSE, AND CHEMICAL LADEN.]

None of it is good! Refined sugars are nutrient-void, calorie dense and chemical laden. This means that your body gains nothing but kilos when you consume it. Refined sugars are very easily digested and absorbed straight into the blood stream, causing elevated blood glucose levels. High blood glucose levels put an enormous strain on your body's system and organs. Subsequently, we can experience weight gain, diabetes and tooth decay, to name just a few.

Not only that, but sugar is highly addictive. It can be hard to stop eating it once you get started. It is very difficult just to eat one candy or one cookie, and it is very easy to eat an excess amount. The more we eat, the more we become acclimated to high levels and the more we want. Processed sugars also disrupt the environment in our guts, specifically altering the delicate balance of "good" bacteria and "bad" bacteria. This can lead to digestive distress and inflammatory symptoms like fatigue, body aches and joint problems, and can worsen pre-existing inflammatory or autoimmune conditions.

Sugar, Sugar Everywhere

Most packaged foods we eat are loaded with sugar. Even the savoury or healthy foods that we think don't contain sugar actually do. This includes ready-made sauce and salad dressing, bread, breakfast cereal, muesli bars, potato chips, diet food, low fat food, the list goes on. When you start to look at the labels on products more closely, you will be surprised. Sugar is like air. It is everywhere!

By quitting processed foods, you will actually also be cutting out refined sugar. You may wonder how on earth it might be possible because you have such a sweet tooth. But sugar feeds sugar cravings. If you are not eating it you will not want it … in time.

The other good news is that nature has provided us with many beautiful sweet treats, so you will never miss out. I share with you some of my favourite desserts and treats made from real food ingredients in the recipe section under sweets and treats.

Grains and Grain Products

Grains are not what they used to be. Although many people believe that "whole" grains are natural and healthy, most grain products have to go through extensive processing before they end up on your plate. Bread, pasta and other flour-based foods found at the grocery store also contain a lot of extra processed ingredients that qualify them as processed foods. This includes gluten free bread and pasta products.

Grains are a controversial topic because we have all been conditioned to think that these foods are the staple of our existence. After all, they are on the base of the food pyramid which we grew up with.

The book *Wheat Belly* by Dr William Davis is one that I recommend you read to learn more about this topic. It is very interesting and goes into a lot more detail about the evolution of grains and why over-processing and genetically modified grains do not agree with our bodies anymore.

Modern grains, in particular wheat, have been created through genetic manipulation to create short, stubby, hardy, high-yielding wheat plants with much higher amounts of starch and gluten. Why would they do this? It is more profitable.

Modern wheat and grains, as we know them, contain super starch and super gluten which is much more likely to create inflammation in the body. Wheat raises blood sugar higher than nearly all other foods, including refined sugar. ☞

Soy

Soy is marketed and also widely thought of as a healthy alternative to dairy. Many people have moved away from cow's milk and drink soy instead, but is it actually a healthy alternative? How do they make soybeans into milk or tofu? They do this through high factory processing, of course.

Soy can be found in almost all processed foods; it is often hidden as soybean oil, soy protein, soy flour, soy fibre, soy albumin, soya, lecithin, textured vegetable protein, vegetable gum, thickener, stabilizer, flavouring and gums. None of these represent real food.

Seed Oils

The seed oil industry is very tricky. The likes of canola oil (from rapeseed), safflower oil, sunflower oil, peanut oil, soya bean oil, flaxseed oil, grape seed oil, and bran oil sound like they are all made from natural ingredients. And you would be right in thinking that because they are, but there is a big but!

The problem with these oils is that they are completely unnatural. Vegetable and seed oils were never available to humans until the 20th century because we simply didn't have the technology to extract them. Unlike coconut or olive oil, you can't just squeeze oil out of a sunflower seed or rice bran. The way these oils are manufactured is disgusting. It involves a harsh extraction process that includes bleaching, deodorizing, and the highly toxic solvent hexane. It is actually amazing that these oils are even edible.

[IT IS ACTUALLY AMAZING THAT THESE OILS ARE EVEN EDIBLE.]

These oils are used at fast food joints and in most processed foods, because it is very cost effective and to make food this way. If you want to quit eating processed foods, you will need to stay away from all of these oils.

Dairy

Lactose is not well tolerated by many people. Even if it's seemingly unnoticeable, removing lactose from your diet can make a big difference to the way you feel and look.

The fat in milk, which is cream and butter, does not contain lactose, so humans can more easily tolerate it.

The other issue with dairy in relation to a real food pledge is that unless you live on a farm and can get milk straight from a cow, milk isn't really milk anymore. Gosh, it is really quite scary isn't it?

Like so much of our food, milk has been tampered with and processed before it arrives at your table. Sugar is added, as well as many other unhealthy additives, to make it last longer and look whiter.

There is a false belief that if you don't drink milk, you will not receive enough calcium.

Milk is not the only food that is rich in calcium. When you eat a diet of real food you will get calcium from eggs, nuts, seeds, fruit, vegetables and seafood. Do not fear.

I personally don't consume much in the way of dairy, except for butter if I have made it myself, and I will also eat carefully selected cheese. I have switched to drinking black tea and coffee, as I no longer drink milk. I feel much better for it.

I suggest leaving dairy at the door for 28 days while you are testing a real food lifestyle.

After you have completed your first 28 days eating only real food, you could try to introduce some unprocessed dairy to see how your body reacts.

White Potatoes and Rice

White potatoes and rice are both natural and real foods. Rice is a grain and does not contain the harmful glutenous proteins that other grains do.

For 28 days, you are going to be saying goodbye to these white loves of your life. White potatoes and rice will be a no-go zone; sorry to be the deliverer of bad news, but here is why...

I have lumped rice and white potatoes together because they are fairly similar in many ways.

- Neither of these foods are nutrient dense and they are both quite high in starchy carbs that send your blood sugar levels soaring.
- Eating white rice and potatoes tends to replace other more nutritious foods such as meat and vegetables on your plate. You are better off filling up on foods that deliver goodness to your cells.
- The starches in rice and potatoes are complex carbohydrates, which your body breaks down into glucose. This happens very quickly, resulting in a more rapid increase in the level of glucose in your bloodstream, which over the next 28 days you are going to work at stabilising.
- Potatoes are used in very bad ways, which we all love, but we really need to stop. Fries, hashbrowns and crisps are all made to pull you in because of their salty, fatty yumminess. None of these are supportive of good health.
- Rice is also used in non-productive ways such as fried rice and sushi. When store-bought, these products are laden with toxic refined sugar and fats.
- If one of the reasons that you want to cut processed food is to lose a few pounds, then potatoes and rice are most certainly not part of that plan. They do not support weight loss.

Personally, I don't eat either rice or potatoes as a general rule, except on the odd occasion if I am served potato while out, then I will eat it and I will enjoy it. I especially enjoy the potatoes that my friend Nicola makes roasted in coconut oil. They are an amazing and delightful treat that I savour. ◆

DON'T BE FOOLED!

There are sneaky ways that food manufacturers trick you into thinking their food is healthy. Often, we try hard to be healthy and we purposefully make healthier choices.

Food companies know their products aren't healthy, and as we have all started to become health conscious, manufacturers need to make sure that we are still going to buy their products. So, they slap a claim on the box that makes the product look healthy. Be aware!

All Natural

Well, this sounds good, since this is what real food is all about – being "all natural". You have probably seen claims that "this food is all natural" or "straight from Mother Nature".

The truth about this is that there are no requirements set forth by food regulators to define what "all natural" food is. Foods with refined grains, high fructose corn syrup, hydrogenated oils and artificial sweeteners can be labelled as all natural.

Call me crazy, but something tells me that chemically extracted oil doesn't grow on trees. Really it is about using common sense when it comes to looking at the ingredients list.

Do not be fooled by large lettering on the front of packages stating the product is "natural".

DO NOT BE FOOLED BY LARGE LETTERING ON THE FRONT OF PACKAGES STATING THE PRODUCT IS "NATURAL".

Look just a little bit deeper to determine if it is really natural or not.

Sugar Free, No Sugar Added or 100% Natural Cane Sugar

Refined and fake sugar is one of our biggest enemies. Beware of labels that claim to be sugar free, no sugar added or 100% natural cane sugar.

Foods that claim to be sugar free or have no added sugars often contain artificial sweeteners or man-made sugar alcohols. Sugar alcohols are far from natural.

Low Fat or Fat-Free

This is just another marketing scam to get people to think they are eating healthier foods. More often, the fat-free version of a product and the regular version have about the same or close to the same amount of calories because the fat is replaced with sugar and other fillers to make the product taste good.

Made with Real Fruit

"Made with real fruit" implies that you're getting nutritional value from the product you're eating. It is made from oranges so it is full of vitamin C.

Not even freshly squeezed orange juice from the supermarket can be trusted to actually be made from oranges. If one of the ingredients is "fruit juice concentrate", it's not a fruit. It's just sugar. You are better off skipping these products and just eating real fruit.

How to Avoid These Tricks and Traps

It is easy to fall into these traps; that's why food companies use them.

The best way to avoid all of these marketing tricks is to read the nutritional labels and ingredients lists when you are grocery shopping. Or you can do what I do – don't purchase any foods that are in packets.

Just buy real food ingredients such as fruit, vegetables, meat, eggs, seafood, nuts and good fats such as coconut and olive oil. ◆

REAL FOOD GUIDELINES

This is the part you have been waiting for! You may be wondering what you will be eating if you choose to embark on this real food lifestyle. You will be eating amazing, tasty, lip smacking real food. For food to be "real" in my definition, it must comply with the following:

It has to be made by nature.

It has to be something that can be made in your kitchen with real food ingredients made by nature.

Contain no refined or artificial sugar of any type.

Contain no grains.

Contain zero hydrogenated oils or polyunsaturated oils.

Be nutrient dense and support your health, not be detrimental to your health.

Food can either strengthen you or it can weaken you! ☞

GET YOUR CYLINDERS REVVING ON REAL FOOD

The benefits of quitting processed food and eating real food for life are amazing. Not only will you be running high on energy, you will also look good and feel fabulous. Here are some very encouraging benefits that I hope will excite you to start your real food pledge.

1 **Real Food Is Rich in Nutrients –** When you eliminate high calorie, nutrient-void processed foods that fill you up (like breads, pasta and sugars), you have space in your food intake to eat loads of protein-rich meats, seafood, eggs, vegetables, healthy fats, nuts, seeds, berries and fruit – all of which are full of minerals and vitamins. Combine that with the improved gut health and increased nutrient absorption, and you will feel and look healthier than you ever have before (in no time at all).

2 **Sustained Weight Loss –** Weight loss is often increased when you eat real food and keep an active lifestyle. Improved metabolic processes and gut health, better sleep, stress management, sufficient Vitamin D and a healthy ratio of Omega-3/6 fatty acids all aid in burning off stored body fat.

3 **Reduced Bloating and Gas –** I was bloated for years, so much so that I couldn't differentiate between being bloated and not being bloated. When I cut out processed foods, this stopped. When you eat real food, you naturally eat lots of fibre, which together with adequate water intake and a smaller intake of sodium, helps to decrease bloating.

4 **Regular Bowel Activity –** A processed, low fat diet in some people promotes constipation and stomach spasms. For me, going to the bathroom was at least a 15 minute task, and it was irregular. Since I have cut out processed foods, I am one of those enviable people who goes every morning at 8:43 on the dot and I am done in a flash! I can then get on with the day with a happy tummy.

5 **Say Goodbye to Hangry –** Have you heard of "hangry"? It is a combination of hungry+angry. This can happen when the blood sugar drops and the person gets a rapid onset of hunger accompanied by irritability, fatigue, disorientation and a foggy mind. Meals consisting of vegetables, protein and fat are very satiating. The energy your body gets from real food is released slowly and evenly throughout the day. As a result, the blood sugar levels stay stable and hunger develops gradually. No more hitting the wall!

OTHER BENEFITS MANY PEOPLE EXPERIENCE FROM EATING REAL FOOD INCLUDE:

- Increased and more stable energy levels
- Improved sleep
- Clearer skin and healthier looking hair
- Mental clarity
- Improved mood and attitude
- Improvements in those suffering depression or anxieties
- Less or no bloating, decreased gas
- Sustained weight loss
- Lowered risk of heart disease, diabetes and cancer
- Higher immune function and a general feeling of well-being
- Healthier gut flora
- Better absorption of nutrients from food
- Reduced allergies
- Reduction of pain associated with inflammation
- Improvements in those with respiratory problems, such as asthma
- Reduced symptoms of menopause

What's in and what's out...

Real Foods That You Can Enjoy:

- Vegetables
- Meat – beef, pork, lamb, venison, kangaroo
- Poultry – chicken, duck, quail, turkey
- Fish, seafood, sea vegetables
- Eggs
- Fruit and berries
- Nuts and seeds
- Spices and herbs
- Healthy Fats – coconut oil, olive oil, avocado oil

Foods to Avoid:

- Processed food – all types
- Breads, cakes, biscuits
- Breakfast cereals – Weet-bix, cornflakes, muesli, etc.
- Canned food – unless no additives
- Grains, especially anything with gluten
- Refined sugars
- Dairy
- Industrial oils – canola, sunflower, rice bran, etc.

Every time you eat, you have the ability to hurt or heal your body. Ask yourself: Is this food going to nourish my body?

WHAT DOES A Real Food Day LOOK LIKE?

Once you get a handle on a real food lifestyle, it becomes very easy and also amazingly delicious. Your day may start with a two-egg omelette with fresh parsley and thyme, topped with smashed avocado. You might have a glass of freshly squeezed carrot, apple and beetroot juice. For lunch, you could enjoy a poached chicken waldorf salad with apple and walnuts. Dinner could be a cut of your favourite variety of beefsteak with roasted carrots, beets and sweet potato with a sprinkling of rosemary and sea salt. Dessert might be homemade raspberry sorbet to cleanse your palate.

How delicious does that day sound? When you eat real food, you have a totally different relationship with food. It is one of respect and love of food in a way that you won't have experienced before. You will never feel guilty about what you put in your mouth ever again. Imagine that sort of freedom!

You won't be hungry between your meals because your blood sugar levels will be stable, and you will not find yourself hunting and sifting around looking for a snack at 10am and then again at 3pm.

It may seem like the "in" list is small, but you are so wrong. You can create amazing, wonderful dishes from the "in" food list just as I have done in the recipe section of this book. There are hundreds of fresh flavours available to you from the "in" list.

[YOU WILL NEVER MISS OUT AND YOU WILL FEEL AND LOOK AMAZING ON THE INSIDE AND OUT.]

Say Goodbye to Processed Foods FOR GOOD

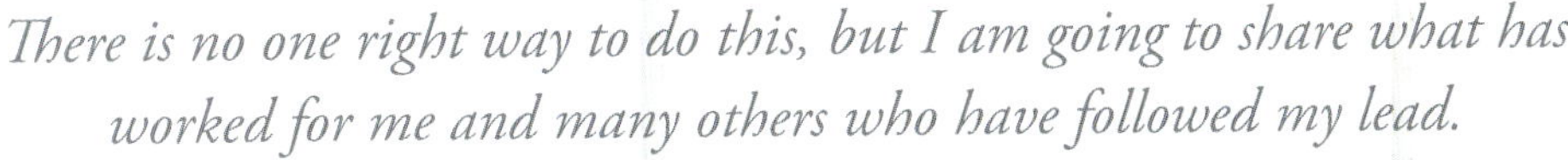

There is no one right way to do this, but I am going to share what has worked for me and many others who have followed my lead.

[TO GET STARTED...]

1 Commit to a 28-day "trial". You don't have to commit beyond that if you don't want to. It is only 4 weeks of your life, and you never know, you may actually like it so much that you commit to cutting out processed foods for life, just like I have.

2 Do it with a friend or co-worker. Do it with someone you know who also wants to commit to a real food pledge. It is much easier if you have a support person whom you are accountable to. You can swap meal ideas and chat about what works for you and what doesn't. My whole office has got on board and it has been fun!

3 Become empowered through reading. There are so many amazing books and resources available. Read and learn as much information as you can on the science and politics of processed foods. It will confirm over and over why you are choosing to switch to real foods. On page 128 is a list of recommended reading for some inspiration on where to start.

4 Explore. Go into your local health food store that you may never have been to, explore your local farmers markets, read new cookbooks, sift around websites that inspire you to cook real food and try new ingredients. On page 123 is a list of ingredients for you to try.

5 Clean up and stock up. Throw away all the processed foods in your house. Seriously! Make sure that you have all the real food ingredients you need on hand to make the food you will be eating.

6 If you have good food in your fridge, you will eat good food. It is really that simple.

7 Don't be hard on yourself. If you commit to exclusively eating real food but mess up from time to time, don't beat yourself up! It is a lifestyle, a journey and a life-long commitment. It is not a fad diet that if you fail you have to start over again. The nutrition police won't arrest you. You will find yourself in situations where you have no choice but to eat processed food, such as on a long flight. But next time you travel, you can be prepared with some of your own real food snacks. Just relax about it and know that you are trying your best. Don't throw in the towel if you "failed", because you didn't!

DISCOVERING YOUR TASTE BUDS

There are about 10,000 taste buds on your tongue. Each one has a receptor that reacts to different substances and makes it possible for you to taste the foods you eat. There are five elements of taste: sour, bitter, salty, savoury and sweet.

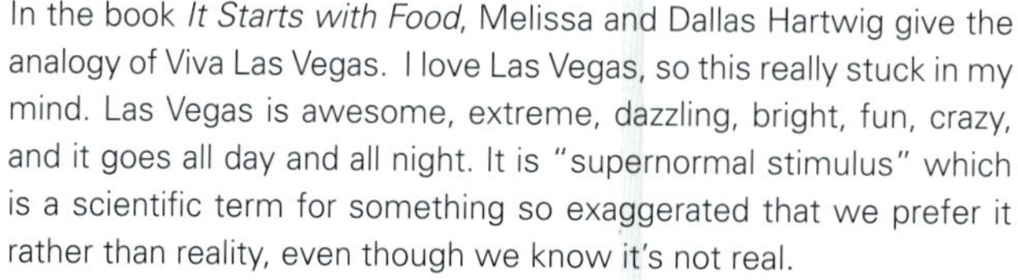

In the book *It Starts with Food*, Melissa and Dallas Hartwig give the analogy of Viva Las Vegas. I love Las Vegas, so this really stuck in my mind. Las Vegas is awesome, extreme, dazzling, bright, fun, crazy, and it goes all day and all night. It is "supernormal stimulus" which is a scientific term for something so exaggerated that we prefer it rather than reality, even though we know it's not real.

Eating fake food is just like Las Vegas. It arouses our taste receptors more intensely than anything found in nature. The Hartwig's give the examples that candy is far sweeter than fruit, sweet and sour pork is far sweeter, saltier and fattier than actual pork. Then they give the example of chocolate bars and cookies, which out-compete against anything in nature. These foods are supernormal stimuli and are just like the Strip in Las Vegas, which is not at all realistic. They dazzle and excite your taste buds. They overwhelm your senses and you find it hard to eat natural foods, because amongst other deeper reasons, you prefer the taste of processed food. When our taste buds are used to these fake, over stimulating foods, natural foods taste bland, dull and boring.

Once you have had a period of time without fake, cheap processed foods, your taste buds will adjust and real food will start to taste really amazing. Berries will zing in your mouth, steak will melt, pork will crackle, and your taste buds will be dazzled again...but by real food.

[BERRIES WILL ZING IN YOUR MOUTH, STEAK WILL MELT, PORK WILL CRACKLE, AND YOUR TASTE BUDS WILL BE DAZZLED AGAIN.]

TIPS TO HELP YOU *On Your Real Food* JOURNEY

Before you start on your 28-day discovery of real food, there are some practical things that you can do to help yourself along:

Be prepared.

Just like a good brownie (not a chocolate brownie, but a girl guide brownie!).

Go to your local green grocer, butcher and farmers market, and stock up on all of the fresh fruit, vegetables and meats that you need. Plan your meals for the week including your breakfasts and lunches, so that you don't get drawn into making processed food choices.

Plan protein packed meals.

Make sure that your meals are packed full of protein, vegetables and healthy fats, so that you stay full for longer and maintain a stable blood sugar. This will prevent you from thinking about processed food and reaching for chips or chocolate.

Play the "food swapping" game.

Think outside the box and swap all of the usual processed foods for real food options. Examples of this are to swap:

- Wheat flour for coconut flour
- Sugar or golden syrup for honey or dates
- Cow's milk for almond or coconut milk
- Chips for homemade salted nuts
- Store bought juice for fresh vegetable or fruit juice
- Soda for mineral water and lime
- Lollies for fresh berries

Experiment in the kitchen.

Start having some fun in the kitchen and make some recipes using real food ingredients. Make real food breakfasts, salads, dinners, desserts and snacks. You can just about convert any recipe into a real food recipe; it doesn't always work out, but it is fun to make new discoveries.

Be organised.

If you know you are going somewhere that will not provide real food options, be organised and take your own. Some of these places might be football games, the movies, flights and fairs. Make some raw chocolate treats, pack some nuts or take a banana.

Be a flavour goddess.

Stock up on fresh herbs, or better yet, grow fresh herbs. Stock up on flavoursome items like spices, vanilla pods, cinnamon, frozen berries and cacao. ◆

TIPS FOR PLANNING Your Real Food Week

You will have to be organised, maybe no more organised than you are now, but just in a different way. I actually visit the store less now than I ever have, which suits me because I am busy. Before I switched to a real food lifestyle, either my husband or I would pop into the grocery store every day on the way home from work. This was incredibly inconvenient! Here are some tips to make planning for a real food week easier:

On the weekend, go to your local farmers market and stock up on all the fresh fruit and vegetables that you need for the week ahead.

❧

Go to the best local butcher that you can afford and stock up on quality meats for the week ahead.

❧

Make some pre-prepared meals for the week such as the Lime Chilli Chicken Tacos, Thai Pumpkin Soup or Sweet Potato Cottage Pie from the recipes in this book. You can freeze these meals and pull them out as you need them.

❧

Make dinner for two nights. For example, make a huge pot of pork and coconut meatballs. For the following night make tacos out of the meatballs.

❧

Make sure that you have a fully stocked fridge. If you have good food, you will eat good food. It's that simple!

❧

Have some take away or fast food options up your sleeve that are healthy. Our local take away food that we enjoy if we are in a bind is to buy a roasted chicken and salad from our local carvery. This is a treat that the whole family loves.

Ok, I know what you are thinking: How can I afford to eat real food when processed food is so much cheaper? This is a comment that I often get from people who follow my blog. To be honest, I think that this is a convenient excuse, and I don't buy it!

Personally, I buy for a family of five and I have not noticed much difference in my grocery bill. I used to spend around $250 per week on groceries, which was probably broken down to $50 on fruits and vegetables, $50 on fresh meat and $150 on other groceries. Now my spending looks more like $100 a week on fresh fruits and vegetables, $100 per week on fresh meat and $50 on grocery items such as dates, nuts, frozen berries and a few household items. I literally do not buy packaged food anymore apart from nuts, berries and good quality tinned tomatoes.

You should be spending 90% of your grocery money on fresh fruit, vegetables, eggs, meats, nuts and seeds and 10% on other items you need like toilet paper.

> PLAN YOUR MEALS. THIS IS ESSENTIAL, AS IT WILL SAVE YOU MONEY AND TIME.

HERE ARE SOME STRATEGIES IF YOU ARE WORKING WITH A TIGHT BUDGET:

1 Become resourceful. What I mean is getting back to the basics of cooking, making your own vegetable stock to keep in the fridge, using the bones from a roast chicken, and learn how to make hearty stews from inexpensive cuts of meat and using up leftovers. Make your own soups for lunches during the week and eat leftovers from dinner the night before.

2 Shop at your local farmers markets. Shopping at your local farmers markets is one of the cheapest ways to eat fresh. Not only that, but I find that the food I buy from my farmers market lasts so much longer than what I buy at the supermarket or even local green grocer.

3 Plan your meals. This is essential, as it will save you money and time. One of the weekly meals that I make is a huge pot of mince with a tomato base. For the first night, we have it on zucchini pasta, and the second night we add some curry to it and serve it in a burrito bowl. It works perfectly and provides two cheap and cheerful dinners for the family.

4 Avoid food waste. Don't throw out your leftovers. Use leftovers for lunch the next day or to add to an omelette for breakfast.

5 Get preserving. Take a leaf out of your grandmother's book and start making some of your own fermented vegetables, sauces, stocks, jams and dips. Save old jars and make some preserves. You can buy bulk fruit or vegetables that are over ripe very cheaply.

6 Compare prices. When you are buying real food, dry ingredients such as bulk almonds, chia seeds, almond meal and dates, make sure you check the prices. I recently went to a bulk food store and bought all sorts of ingredients to stock up. I didn't really think too much about it and just bought what I wanted. The next day, I was at my local fruit and vegetable store where they also sell bags of nuts. The almonds were $5.99 for 500 grams. The day before, I was scooping almonds out of the bulk bin for $21.00 per kilo at nearly double the price. ◆

Take a leaf out of your grandmother's book...

CAN I EVER EAT IT AGAIN?

"Chocolate is from cocoa which is a tree. That means it is a plant. Essentially, chocolate is salad!" Don't fear, you can eat chocolate, I told you that you will never miss out!

When you quit processed foods that does mean cutting out all processed foods, including processed chocolate. Most store-bought chocolates are made from cocoa, which is a refined version of cacao. Processed chocolate also contains refined sugar, bad oils and additives. So stay away from this type of chocolate.

I do have good news for you though. Chocolate is made from cacao, and cacao is a richly nutritious super food. It is very easy to make your own chocolate, chocolate desserts and chocolate treats from real food ingredients that actually taste better than store-bought chocolate. Cacao is hugely beneficial for us!

Benefits of Cacao – The Super Food

- Cacao is chock-full of health benefits and could easily be considered one of nature's best medicines.
- Cacao is considered a "super-antioxidant".
- Cacao is a great source of magnesium, which helps with calcium absorption, metabolism and protein synthesis.
- The unprocessed raw cacao earns a higher antioxidant score than spinach, acai berries or blueberries.
- In cacao, the high antioxidant activity helps to protect the heart, prevents cellular damage and keeps us looking and feeling younger.
- Cacao also contains iron, copper, calcium, potassium and zinc. ◆

CHECK OUT THE
TRIPLE CHOCOLATE BLISS BALLS
ON PAGE 110

Eating OUT & ABOUT

EATING OUT IS A REALITY

We all live in the real, modern world and at some point, you are going to eat out. I eat out a lot because of my husband's work and we enjoy eating out on weekends. It is actually easier than you think to avoid highly processed foods while eating out. More and more restaurants are offering healthy real food options.

Here are my tips for eating out:

- Avoid fast food joints. This is as obvious as one would think, but I have to say it anyway. If you do have to go to a fast food joint, a better option would be somewhere you can get grilled chicken, salad or grilled fish.
- Pub menus usually have steak and salad on the menu. Hold the fries and sauces.
- Instead of ordering garlic bread, which used to be mandatory for me, start with oysters or something else divine from the entrée menu.
- If you are going out for breakfast, order simple poached eggs with a side of avocado or mushrooms. Hold the toast. I also find that the chef will fill your plate with extra sides. Avoid dishes like scrambled eggs, muesli or soufflés. Keep it simple.
- Buffets are great; they usually have fresh simple seafood, salads and carved meats. Stay away from the dessert bar. If you must have something for dessert, opt for some nuts or fruit. You can make nicer desserts at home anyway.
- If you are ordering a salad, ask for the dressing to be on the side. You can also request that they bring you a side of olive oil or fresh lemon.
- If there is a club sandwich, Panini or taco on the menu that takes your fancy, ask if they would make it for you without the bread or taco. Most places are accommodating and fill your plate with the main event rather than the space fillers such as the Panini bread.
- Hot rock restaurants are a really great option. Get your meat with a large side of vegetables instead of fries.
- Most mainstream restaurants that you go to for dinner have chicken, fish, beef or pork as a main option served with a vegetable side dish. Most of these will be safe.
- Try your coffee as a long black over ice. Even if you do not enjoy black coffee, you might enjoy it like this.
- Sparkling water is a fabulous option. Ask for it to be topped with mint and lime.
- When you are ordering your food, don't be afraid to ask questions so that you can make informed decisions.

WE ALL LIVE IN THE REAL, MODERN WORLD AND AT SOME POINT, YOU ARE GOING TO EAT OUT.

STAYING ON the Real Food BANDWAGON

This is not a quick fix diet. I cannot stress that enough. This is a lifestyle change.

I am encouraging you to take a real food pledge for 28 days so that you can see the changes in your body for yourself, but the idea is that you make a permanent lifestyle change where you only eat real food.

That is where you will see amazing changes.

My goal for you is that this challenge is a positive one where through your own experimentation, you will learn something new about food and develop some long-term good habits. You will feel good when you are no longer eating processed food, and it is my wish for you that you will continue being a better, healthier version of yourself for the rest of your life.

As I have said throughout this book, we all live in the real world and we have to be realistic. There will be times that being completely free of processed foods is not possible. Examples of this could be going on holiday, travelling, family occasions or going to dinner parties. You might go to a new country and want to try their traditional food that does not comply with your real food philosophy. If I were going to travel to Italy, I would want to try their pizza!

I recently went to China and getting there was a food nightmare for me. The food on the plane was highly processed and the food

> YOU WILL CONTINUE BEING A BETTER, HEALTHIER VERSION OF YOURSELF FOR THE REST OF YOUR LIFE.

at the airport was also limited. It wasn't the end of the world. I just resumed my normal eating once the day was over and I was in a position to have the choice.

In order to be successful in making a positive lifestyle change you need to have realistic goals and expectations for yourself and your special circumstances. You may need to work out some guidelines that are acceptable to you and your life so that you avoid setting yourself up for failure.

When you have been eating a real food diet for a while, you will notice how awful you feel if you then eat processed food. That alone is usually enough to stop me in my tracks. Also, when you are armed with information about how processed food hooks you in and that it is so bad for your health, it is easier to not want it.

Whatever you do, don't beat yourself up. Learn and move on. ◆

OK, SO I HAVE ARMED YOU WITH ENOUGH INFORMATION TO *get you started,* WHAT NEXT?

Over the next 28 days, you are going to join the tribe and pledge to eat real food.

YOUR Real Food PLEDGE

1 Eat real food, which are the foods listed on page 32.

2 Consume no processed foods including foods listed on page 32 or anything with sugar, dairy, grains, industrial oils and alcohol.

3 Read the labels before you purchase any food in packets to make sure all of the ingredients are real food ingredients.

4 Clean out your pantry and fridge to remove any temptations. Then fill your cupboards with lots of fruit, vegetables, meats, seafood, nuts and good fats. If you have good food in your kitchen, you will eat good food.

5 Educate yourself with new ingredients, recipes and real food information.

6

Make you and your family some yummy recipes from this book. My personal favourite is the Lemon Tart.

7

Enjoy experimenting with new ingredients and thinking outside of the processed food square.

8

Pre-prepare yourself some homemade meals such as banana muffins, chicken tacos or seed bread and freeze them so that you have good food to turn to if you find yourself in a hurry.

9

Learn to love herbal tea. Try some new ones; start with ginger or liquorice. Drink raw cacao. Yum!

10

Enjoy your food and the amazing changes that are going to happen. I promise you will feel sparkly, energised and dazzling in 28 days from now. Then keep going!

NOW FOR SOME AMAZING FOOD.

I really hope that you enjoy the recipes I have put together for you as much as I have enjoyed creating them.

There are enough breakfast, lunch, dinner and treat ideas to keep you fuelled on real food for an entire week.

Lauralee xxx

"ALL HAPPINESS DEPENDS ON A
LEISURELY BREAKFAST."
John Gunther

breakfast

When considering a real food lifestyle, sometimes breakfast can be the most challenging for people, simply because our Western culture and mindset tells us that we should eat cereal and toast with sugary toppings for breakfast. I am here to share with you that there are many wonderful real foods that you can enjoy at breakfast time.

You will need to think outside the square, but it is worth it.

This is a delicious and tasty, fruity spin on eggs. I often make this when I am in a hurry because it only takes a few moments to whip up and it is delicious.

berry & coconut OMELETTE

INGREDIENTS

- ½ cup fresh or frozen berries (defrosted)
- 2 eggs
- 2 tablespoons of coconut milk
- ½ teaspoon of coconut oil
- Sprinkle of cinnamon
- Sprinkle of nutmeg
- Drizzle of honey
- Berries to garnish (optional)
- Coconut yoghurt (optional)

DIRECTIONS

In a small bowl, whisk the eggs, coconut milk and a sprinkle of cinnamon and nutmeg until combined.

Heat the coconut oil in a small pan over a medium heat on the stove. Pour the whipped egg mixture into the pan. As the edges cook, shift the egg into the centre, letting the runny egg mixture run out to the edge of the pan. Place the berries on top of the egg in a line through the centre of the egg and let the egg set.

Fold over each side of the egg on top of the berries. Slide the omelette out onto a plate and top with fresh berries, coconut yoghurt and a drizzle of honey.

SERVES 1

Sometimes it is nice to have a comforting and warming piece of toast. This recipe is my go to grain and gluten free bread recipe. It is seriously the yummiest bread I have ever had! You can top it with eggs, tomato, avocado, figs and cashew butter. Two slices keep me fuelled until lunchtime.

seed toast

INGREDIENTS

- 2 tablespoons linseeds
- 2 tablespoons sunflower seeds
- 2 tablespoons chia seeds
- 2 tablespoons pumpkin seeds
- ½ cup warm water
- 1 cup walnuts
- ¼ cup coconut flour
- 1 pinch of salt
- 1 teaspoon baking soda
- 2 tablespoons apple cider vinegar
- 3 eggs
- 2 tablespoons olive or coconut oil

DIRECTIONS

Preheat oven to 180 degrees celsius and line a 23cm loaf tin with baking paper. Soak linseeds, sunflower seeds, pumpkin seeds and chia seeds in the warm water for 5 minutes.

In a food processor add walnuts, coconut flour, baking soda and salt. Process until the mixture resembles fine breadcrumbs. Beat together eggs, oil and vinegar; then add to dry ingredients. Use pulse setting in the food processor until mixed well, being careful not to over mix. Add the seeds and combine. Pour batter into a loaf tin and bake for 25–30 minutes or until a skewer comes out clean.

Serve hot, toast it or wait until the loaf is cool and serve it with your favourite real food toppings. Try avocado with salt and pepper or cashew butter with sliced figs.

MAKES 10 SLICES

I love this dish. It is perfect to make on one of those long, lazy Sunday mornings at home. The beautiful rich flavours are warm, and the eggs and chorizo provide a hearty way to start the day.

baked eggs

WITH CHORIZO, TOMATO & ZUCCHINI

INGREDIENTS

- 4 eggs
- 1 zucchini, diced
- 1 onion, diced
- 3 ripe tomatoes, diced
- ½ chorizo sausage, sliced
- 1 garlic clove, crushed
- 1 sprig fresh thyme
- Pinch of salt
- Pinch of chilli flakes (optional)
- ½ tablespoon olive oil
- Fresh herbs to garnish (optional)

DIRECTIONS

Slice the chorizo and dice the onion, zucchini and tomatoes. In a pan over a medium heat, sauté the garlic and onions in the olive oil until the onion is transparent. Add the chorizo and zucchini, sauté for a further 3 minutes. Add the tomato, thyme, salt and chilli flakes; reduce down for 10 minutes, stirring on occasion. Depending on how juicy your tomatoes are, you may need to add a little water if it looks dry.

Crack the eggs on top of the tomato base. Place a lid on top of the pan, checking the eggs regularly. Remove from stovetop when the eggs are cooked to your liking.

Serve with a sprinkle of fresh herbs, cracked sea salt and pepper.

SERVES 2

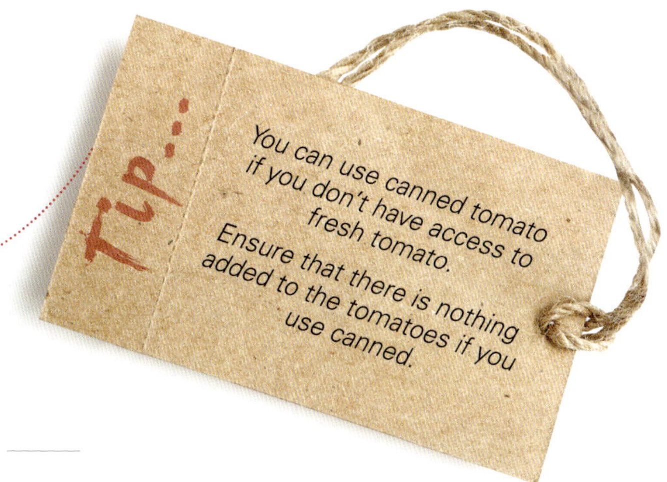

I love a stack of pancakes, there is just something so special about them. These little beauties will satisfy your pancake cravings but they are healthy. You can use left over pumpkin or you can keep some pumpkin puree in the freezer in zip lock bags for when you want to make this recipe.

pumpkin pancakes

INGREDIENTS

- 6 eggs
- ¾ cup pumpkin puree
- 1 teaspoon vanilla extract
- 1 teaspoon cinnamon
- ½ teaspoon nutmeg
- ½ teaspoon cardamom
- 3 tablespoons coconut flour
- ¼ teaspoon baking soda
- 1 pinch salt
- 1 tablespoon of coconut oil

DIRECTIONS

In a large bowl or blender, mix together eggs, pumpkin, vanilla, cinnamon, nutmeg and cardamom. Add the baking soda, salt and coconut flour; mix until combined.

Heat a pan over a medium heat and grease with 1 teaspoon of coconut oil. Pour the batter into the pan to make a pancake. Allow the pancake to cook for a few minutes, and flip it once bubbles start to appear. Cook the other side for 1–2 more minutes. Repeat until all of the batter is made into pancakes.

You could serve them with a side of bacon, fresh berries, coconut yoghurt or natural maple syrup.

SERVES 4

Smoothies are a fantastic option if you are like I am and always in a hurry in the mornings. If you are out of time, you can still eat a nutritious breakfast by whipping this recipe up in two minutes, and then you can drink it in the car on the way to work.

ANTIOXIDANT

berry & mint smoothie

INGREDIENTS

1 cup frozen berries

1 handful of fresh mint leaves

½ cup of almond milk

½ cup of coconut milk

DIRECTIONS

Place all the ingredients in the blender or food processor, and blend until the mixture is lump free.

Top with fresh berries.

SERVES 2

There is no reason why you can't enjoy a beautiful fresh salad for breakfast, and there is no better combination than smoked salmon and eggs. Try this recipe and then add your own spin to it.

Smoked Salmon
BREAKFAST SALAD

INGREDIENTS

- 1 cup chopped cos lettuce and rocket or other salad greens
- 1 handful of cherry tomatoes, halved
- ½ avocado, sliced
- 1 radish, thinly sliced
- 1 slice smoked salmon
- 1 boiled egg
- Olive oil to taste
- Salt and pepper to taste

DIRECTIONS

Lay the rocket and cos lettuce on a serving plate. Place the halved tomatoes, sliced avocado and sliced radish around the plate on top of salad greens. Break up the smoked salmon and layer it over the salad.

To boil the egg to perfection, bring a small pot full of water to the boil. Place the egg in the water to simmer for 6 minutes. Remove the egg after 6 minutes and peel under cool water. Place the peeled egg on top of salad.

Drizzle with the olive oil and season with salt and pepper to taste.

SERVES 1

These muffins make a very filling breakfast or snack on the go. I make these and store them in the freezer so that there is always something nice for breakfast, even if I am in a rush to get out the door in the mornings.

banana & cinnamon MUFFINS

INGREDIENTS

- 1 cup dried dates
- 2 ripe bananas
- ½ cup coconut flour
- 2 teaspoons of cinnamon
- 1 teaspoon of baking soda
- Pinch of salt
- 5 eggs
- 2 tablespoons of coconut oil
- ½ cup of water
- 1 teaspoon of coconut oil (for greasing muffin pans)

DIRECTIONS

Preheat the oven to 180 degrees celsius and grease a medium sized 12-hole muffin pan with coconut oil.

In the food processor, process the dates and coconut flour until it is finely blended. Add the bananas, cinnamon, baking soda and salt; process until combined. Then add the eggs, coconut oil and water, and process until well combined. Pour the batter into the muffin pans and place in the oven. Bake for 20 minutes or until they spring back when you press on the top of them.

Top with fresh banana or serve plain.

MAKES 12 MUFFINS

This is a lovely café style breakfast that you can make on the weekend for your family. I love the combination of sweet potato and avocado with a runny egg oozing over the dish; it is happiness on a plate!

sweet potato hashies

TOPPED WITH AVOCADO & POACHED EGG

INGREDIENTS

- 2 medium sweet potatoes
- 1 small onion
- 1 garlic clove, crushed
- 1 teaspoon olive oil
- 1 sprig of thyme
- 1 teaspoon fresh rosemary
- 1 egg, lightly beaten
- Salt & pepper to taste
- 2 eggs for poaching
- 1 ripe avocado, smashed
- Fresh parsley to garnish
- 1–2 tablespoons coconut oil

DIRECTIONS

Peel the onion and dice finely. Heat a pan on the stove over a medium heat and sauté the onion and garlic with a splash of olive oil until the onion becomes translucent. Peel the sweet potato and grate using a box grater. In a large bowl, place the grated sweet potato, onion, garlic, thyme, rosemary, egg and salt and pepper to taste. Use a fork to combine the ingredients. Heat a large fry pan with a teaspoon of coconut oil, place a heaped tablespoon of the sweet potato mixture in the pan. Let the sweet potato cook and turn golden brown. Turn the sweet potato over once it is golden brown and repeat on the other side.

In a small saucepan, bring some salted water to the boil; crack the two eggs into water to poach. Once the eggs are cooked to your liking, carefully drain the water.

Peel the avocado and cut it in half; then place it on a chopping board. With a fork, smash the avocado and season with salt and pepper.

On a serving plate, place two sweet potato hashies down, top with a dollop of smashed seasoned avocado and carefully place a poached egg on top. Garnish with roughly chopped fresh herbs and salt and pepper to taste.

SERVES 2

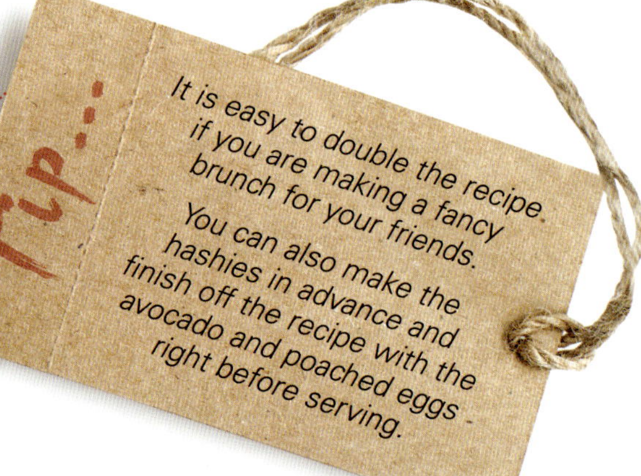

Chia seed puddings are the easiest recipes in the world to make, and they make a nice breakfast that you can enjoy on the go. Chia seeds are packed with goodness including calcium, potassium, vitamin C, omega-3 fatty acids and antioxidants.

chia seed puddings

CHERRY POP CHIA PUDDING

INGREDIENTS

- 3 tablespoons of chia seeds
- 1 cup almond milk
- 1 cup pitted fresh cherries, plus extra for garnish
- ½ teaspoon vanilla extract
- 1 teaspoon of honey
- 1 small pinch of sea salt

DIRECTIONS

In a food processor, blend a cup of pitted fresh cherries until they are smooth. Add almond milk, vanilla, honey and sea salt, and combine. Pour the mixture into a glass jug and add the chia seeds; whisk until there are no lumps. Pour into 3–4 jars or glasses and refrigerate overnight. Decorate with fresh cherries. It keeps in the fridge for up to 3 days.

SERVES 3–4

PIÑA COLADA CHIA PUDDING

INGREDIENTS

- 3 tablespoons of chia seeds
- 1 cup of coconut milk
- ½ cup fresh pineapple, diced
- 2 tablespoons of fresh mint leaves, finely chopped
- 1 teaspoon of honey
- 1 small pinch of sea salt

DIRECTIONS

Dice the pineapple, finely slice the mint leaves and place in a medium glass jug. Add all remaining ingredients and whisk together until there are no lumps. Pour into little jars or glasses and refrigerate overnight. Decorate with mint and diced pineapple. It keeps in the fridge for up to 3 days.

SERVES 3–4

STRAWBERRY, VANILLA & ALMOND CHIA PUDDING

INGREDIENTS

- 3 tablespoons of chia seeds
- 1 cup almond milk
- 1 cup fresh strawberries, sliced, plus extra for garnish
- ¼ cup almond slithers, plus extra for garnish
- ½ teaspoon vanilla extract
- 1 teaspoon of honey
- 1 small pinch of sea salt

DIRECTIONS

In the bottom of 3 – 4 glass jars or glasses, place a layer of strawberry slices and slivered almonds. Whisk together almond milk, chia seeds, vanilla, honey and salt until there are no lumps. Pour into the prepared jars or glasses and refrigerate overnight. Decorate with more strawberries and sliced almonds. It keeps in the fridge for up to 3 days.

SERVES 3–4

"ASK NOT WHAT YOU CAN DO
FOR YOUR COUNTRY.
ASK WHAT'S FOR LUNCH."
Orson Wells

lunch

When you eat real food, it does not have to be boring salads every day. I like to zing it up and enjoy a variety. I have put together for you a few of my favourite lunches that I enjoy.

On the weekend I might make something a little more extravagant like the Orange and Scallop Salad, while during the week I take some soup or tacos to work that I have prepared in advance.

thai pumpkin & coconut
SOUP

INGREDIENTS

- 700 grams of pumpkin
- 1 onion
- 2 cloves of garlic
- 1 teaspoon fresh ginger
- ½ long red chilli
- 1 stem lemon grass
- 1 kaffir lime leaf
- 500 ml of vegetable stock
- ½ cup coconut cream
- 1 handful fresh coriander
- 1 tablespoon of olive oil

DIRECTIONS

Peel and cut the pumpkin into cubes and set aside. Dice the onion and crush the garlic and ginger. In a large saucepan over a medium heat, place the olive oil, onion, ginger and garlic. Sauté for a couple of minutes until the onion is transparent.

Meanwhile, finely slice the kaffir lime leaf, chilli and lemon grass stem, then add to the saucepan. Sauté for a further for 2 minutes with the onion mixture. Add the vegetable stock and pumpkin to the saucepan. Place a lid on the saucepan and simmer for 20 minutes or until the pumpkin is tender. Transfer mixture to a food processor and process until smooth.

Serve in soup dishes and top with a tablespoon of coconut cream and fresh coriander.

SERVES 4–6

This salad is so crunchy and delicious. The flavours go together perfectly and it is very simple to throw these ingredients together in a hurry for a nourishing lunch.

fennel, apple & walnut SALAD

INGREDIENTS

½ fennel bulb, sliced

1 red apple, sliced

½ cup raw walnuts, halved

1 handful of fresh coriander

3 tablespoons olive oil

3 tablespoons of juice of lemon

1 garlic clove, crushed

Salt and pepper to taste

DIRECTIONS

Cut the fennel bulb in half and take the core out. Cut one half into quarters and slice finely across the bulb, then place in a large salad bowl. Cut the apple into quarters and remove the core, leaving the skin on for some colour. Slice the apple finely and place in the salad bowl. Add the walnuts and a handful of coriander leaves. Combine all the ingredients.

To make the dressing, combine the lemon juice, olive oil and crushed garlic in a jar or shaker.

Shake together and drizzle over the salad.

SERVES 4

Frittatas make very tasty meals for any time of the day. They are also a great way to use up leftovers that you may have in the fridge. This recipe is really easy to make and is packed with nutritious vegetables.

Vegetable frittata

INGREDIENTS

1 cup pumpkin, sliced

1 medium onion, sliced

1 medium zucchini, sliced lengthwise

½ red capsicum, sliced

1 cup mushrooms, sliced

1 medium tomato, sliced

7 sprigs asparagus

1 sprig parsley, chopped

1 sprig thyme, chopped

6 eggs, lightly whisked

Salt and pepper to taste

1 tablespoon olive oil

DIRECTIONS

Preheat oven to 180 degrees celsius. Grease a 20cm diameter baking dish with a drizzle of olive oil and line the base with baking paper. Cook the pumpkin in a saucepan of water until just tender.

Meanwhile, heat the olive oil in large frying pan and sauté the onion, zucchini, mushrooms, asparagus and capsicum for 3 minutes until just tender. Layer all the ingredients (except the asparagus) including the tomato and fresh thyme in the prepared baking dish.

In a small dish, lightly whisk the eggs, salt, pepper and parsley together. Pour the egg mixture over the vegetables. Place in the oven and bake for 30 minutes or until cooked through. Garnish with fresh herbs and the asparagus sprigs.

Stand for 5 minutes and then serve.

SERVES 4–6

This is a beautiful lunch and it is just a little bit fancy if you want to treat yourself to some lovely fresh scallops.

orange & scallop SALAD

INGREDIENTS

- 10 scallops
- 2 oranges
- 1 cup fennel
- 1 cup red cabbage
- ¼ cup sliced almonds
- 3 sprigs coriander
- 1 tablespoon coconut oil
- 1 clove crushed garlic

Orange Dressing

- 1/3 cup orange juice
- 2 tablespoons white vinegar
- 1 teaspoon of honey
- 3 tablespoons of olive oil
- Pinch of salt and pepper
- Drizzle olive oil

DIRECTIONS

Drain the scallops and let them dry in between 2 pieces of paper hand towel. Peel the oranges, removing the skin and pith, then slice. Slice the fennel and red cabbage. On two plates, lay out the fennel, red cabbage and orange slices. Toast the almonds by heating a small pan on the stove over a medium heat with a tiny drizzle of olive oil. Lightly roast the almonds for a couple of minutes. Sprinkle the almonds around the plate.

For the scallops, heat a frying pan on the stove over a medium heat. Place the coconut oil and garlic in the pan. Once the garlic starts to sizzle, place the scallops in the pan and let them caramelise, which will take a couple of minutes. Turn and caramelise the other side of the scallops for 2 or 3 minutes. Remove from the pan and place 5 scallops around each of the salads. Garnish with the coriander.

To make the dressing, squeeze 2 oranges to yield 1/3 cup of juice. In a shaker place all the ingredients and shake briskly until combined. Drizzle over the salad.

SERVES 2

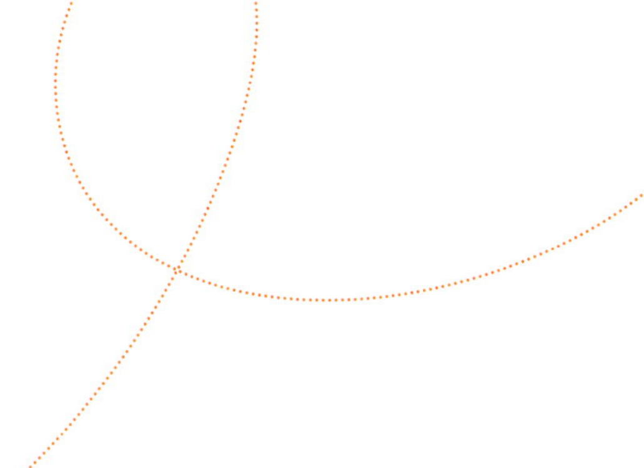

I love this type of meal because it is so simple but tastes, as well as looks, amazing. This is a fabulous idea for a weekend lunch, and it is the perfect crowd pleaser.

sweet potato sliders

INGREDIENTS

- 1–2 large sweet potatoes (16 slices required)
- 300 grams beef mince
- 1 handful of fresh coriander
- 1 clove garlic, crushed
- ½ small onion, diced
- Pinch of salt and pepper
- 1 avocado, sliced
- 2 tomatoes, sliced
- 4 cherry tomatoes, halved
- 3 lettuce leaves
- 1 tablespoon coconut oil

DIRECTIONS

Preheat the oven to 180 degrees celsius and line a baking tray with baking paper. Peel the sweet potato and slice rounds of approximately 4–5mm thick. Place rounds on baking tray and spray with olive oil and sprinkle with sea salt. Bake until golden brown and cooked through, which will take around 15–20 minutes.

To make the mini beef burgers, place the mince in a large bowl with the crushed garlic, diced onion, fresh coriander and some salt and pepper to taste. With your hands or a fork, combine the ingredients, then press the meat mixture into 8 patties. Heat a large pan over a medium heat and grease with a teaspoon of coconut oil. Place the patties in the pan and cook until golden brown on each side.

Slice the avocado and tomato and cut the lettuce to the right size. Assemble the sliders and hold together with skewers.

MAKES 8

This is a fantastic option for lunch or for a quick dinner-time meal. This is one of my kids' favourite meals because they love to build their own tacos. If I cook this meal for them, I just hold the chilli.

lime chicken tacos

INGREDIENTS

1 large chicken breast cooked and shredded

1 onion

2 cloves garlic

3 ripe tomatoes

1 teaspoon of chilli powder (optional)

1 teaspoon of ground turmeric

1 teaspoon of ground cumin seeds

1 teaspoon of paprika

Pinch of salt

1 tablespoon olive oil

1 lime, juiced

1 handful of fresh coriander

8 cos or romaine lettuce leaves

1 avocado, diced

1 tomato, diced

DIRECTIONS

Slice the onion and crush the garlic. Heat a large pan on a medium heat with the olive oil and sauté the onion and garlic until it becomes translucent.

In the meantime, dice up the ripe tomatoes then place in the pan. Let simmer for 3 minutes, then add the chilli, turmeric, cumin, paprika and salt. Stir ingredients together then let simmer for a further 5 minutes stirring on occasion. Add the shredded chicken and combine all the ingredients and allow to simmer for 5 more minutes. Turn off the heat and squeeze the juice from the lime over the mixture.

Wash and prepare the cos lettuce. Fill each lettuce leaf with lime chilli chicken and top with fresh tomato, avocado and fresh coriander.

SERVES 4

This has been my go to lunch for years. It doesn't take long to throw together and is full of fresh yumminess! I went to Chang Mai in North Thailand and spent two days at cooking school which was an amazing experience. I learned how to cook a range of traditional Thai dishes, which taught me how to incorporate those beautiful Thai flavours into my every day meals.

thai beef salad

ON CARROT SLAW

INGREDIENTS

- 200 grams beef steak
- 1 onion
- 1 clove of garlic, crushed
- 1 knob of fresh ginger, crushed
- 1 teaspoon coconut oil
- ½ long red chilli, sliced
- 1 teaspoon of honey
- 2 tablespoons of fish sauce
- 3 tablespoons of fresh lime juice
- 1 carrot
- 1 cup sliced red cabbage
- 1 handful fresh basil
- 1 handful of fresh coriander

DIRECTIONS

To start, peel the carrot and julienne, finely slice the red cabbage and roughly chop the basil along with the coriander. Place all the salad ingredients in a large bowl and combine.

Slice the beefsteak into long strips. Heat a large pan over a medium heat and add the oil. Add the beef strips and sear each side of the strips for 1 minute. Be careful not to overcook the beef. Set the beef aside in a bowl. In the hot pan add the crushed garlic, crushed ginger, sliced chilli and onion. Stir fry for 2 minutes. In a small dish, mix together the lime juice, honey and fish sauce. Add the steak strips back into the pan. Add the sauce mixture over the steak. Stir fry for a couple of minutes being careful not to overcook the steak.

Assemble the carrot slaw in two separate bowls, place the steak and sauce on the top of the slaw. To finish, garnish with fresh coriander

SERVES 2

"A MAN SELDOM THINKS WITH MORE
EARNESTNESS OF ANYTHING
THAN HE DOES OF HIS DINNER."
Samuel Johnson

dinner

Dinner for me is all about spending time with my family.

We eat at the table every night and chat about our days. I have the boys trained to set the table and clean up after we finish, so it is pretty good these days!

All the meals that I have shared with you are recipes that I cook at home all the time. They are simple and quick, but very tasty.

At our house we have salmon for dinner at least once a week. I find that it is a really simple dish to make when I am pressed for time at the end of the day. I really love the summery flavours of this dish when it is served with the fresh mango and avocado salad.

crispy skin salmon

WITH MANGO & AVOCADO SALAD

INGREDIENTS

4 salmon steaks (skin on and all the same size)

1 tablespoon olive oil

Pinch of salt and pepper

Mango & Avocado Salad

1 mango

1 avocado

½ long red chilli

1 cup of coriander

½ lemon (juice)

1 tablespoon of olive oil

Salt and pepper to taste

DIRECTIONS

Heat a large pan on the stove over a medium heat. Add the oil and once it is hot, place the salmon fillets in the pan skin side down. Sprinkle with salt and pepper to taste. After 5 minutes the skin should be crispy; turn the salmon to brown the other side. It depends how large your fillets are as to how long you will need to cook them. I work on 4 or 5 minutes per side and I like the salmon still pink in the middle. Remove from the pan and serve with the mango and avocado salad.

Mango & Avocado Salad

Peel both the avocado and mango. Cut the cheeks away from the mango and dice the flesh. Remove the stone from the avocado and dice, keeping the diced cubes to a similar size as the diced mango. Place the diced mango and avocado in a large bowl. Finely slice the red chilli and roughly chop the coriander. Add to the bowl. Juice the lemon into the salad and add along with the olive oil and salt and pepper to taste. Combine all the ingredients with a fork. Serve with the crispy skin salmon.

SERVES 4

This is a more traditional type of dish that I grew up with. However, this version is much healthier and more nourishing. I love this dish, it is really warming and comforting, just like a hug on your plate!

SWEET POTATO cottage pie

INGREDIENTS

500 grams of beef mince
1 onion
1 garlic clove
1 large carrot
1 large zucchini
¼ cup frozen peas
1 teaspoon curry powder
½ teaspoon paprika
1 cup vegetable stock
Salt to taste
1 tablespoon olive oil
500 grams sweet potato
2 tablespoons olive oil for mash (optional)

DIRECTIONS

Peel the sweet potato and cut each sweet potato into 4 pieces. Place in a pot of boiling water with the lid on and let simmer for 20 minutes.

In the meantime, dice the onion, garlic and carrots. Heat a large pan on a medium heat with the olive oil. Sauté the diced vegetables for a few minutes. Add the mince and cook in the pan for a few minutes. In the meantime, grate the zucchini, then add to the mince along with the peas, curry powder and paprika. When the mince is browned, add the stock and stir to combine. Let the mince simmer on the stove for 20 minutes, or until the stock has reduced right down. Add salt to taste to your liking if need be.

Once the sweet potato is cooked, remove it from the stove and drain off the water. Add the olive oil, salt and pepper, then mash with a potato masher or in your food processor. Place the mince mixture into an oven dish, draining excess juice off. Top with the sweet potato mash and smooth out the top.

Place in the oven at 180 degrees celsius and bake until the top is slightly brown which will take approximately 15–20 minutes. Top with fresh herbs just before serving.

SERVES 6

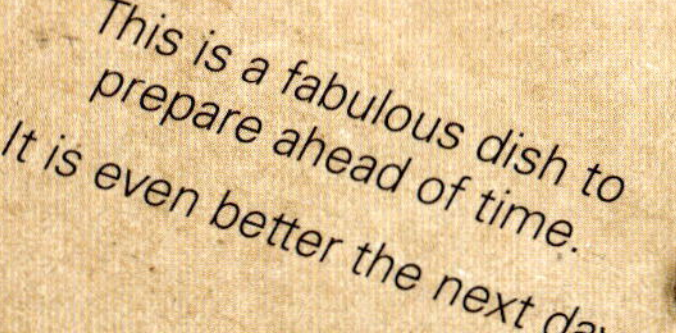

Pork and apple are one of my all-time favourite combinations. This dish is something that I cook regularly for my family, and we all love it. The apple and onion chutney also goes very well with a pork roast.

pork chops
WITH APPLE & ONION CHUTNEY

INGREDIENTS

- 4 pork chops (bone in)
- 2 apples, sliced
- 1 onion, sliced
- 2 cloves garlic, crushed
- ¼ cup unsweetened sultanas
- 1 teaspoon fresh ginger, crushed
- ¼ teaspoon dry mustard powder
- ½ tablespoon apple cider vinegar
- ½ teaspoon ground pepper
- ½ teaspoon sea salt
- 3 tablespoon olive oil

Cauliflower Mash

- ½ head cauliflower (stalks and all)
- 2 tablespoons olive oil
- Salt and pepper to taste
- Pinch of chilli powder (optional)

DIRECTIONS

Peel and slice the apples. Cut the onion in half, remove the outer layer and slice. Heat 2 tablespoons of olive oil in a saucepan over a medium heat. Place the onion, apple, sultanas, crushed ginger, crushed garlic, ground mustard, pepper and salt in the saucepan. Cook for a few minutes, stirring as needed. Add the apple cider vinegar. Continue to cook the chutney for a further 5–10 minutes until all the liquid is reduced.

In the meantime, heat 1 tablespoon of olive oil in a large pan over a medium heat. Place the pork chops down in the pan and cook for 5 minutes on each side. Once the pork is cooked and caramelised on each side, serve with the apple and onion chutney on the top.

The time may vary depending on the thickness of the pork chops.

Cauliflower Mash

The trick to making a good cauliflower mash is to steam the cauliflower so that it is not too watery. Bring to the boil a large saucepan of water (the saucepan needs to fit a steamer). Cut the cauliflower into pieces and include the stalks, place in the steamer, and put the lid on. Steam for 20 minutes or until the cauliflower is tender. Once cooked, place the cauliflower into the food processor, along with the olive oil, salt and pepper. Blitz until very smooth. You can mash it by hand, but it is very hard to get a smooth consistency.

Serve the mash with a sprinkle of chilli.

SERVES 4

prawn skewers

WITH GARLIC & HONEY GLAZE

INGREDIENTS

500 grams of green king prawns

1 clove garlic, crushed

1 tablespoon of honey

2 tablespoons of coconut aminos

½ long red chilli finely sliced

1 tablespoon fresh lime juice

1 tablespoon coconut oil

Lychee & Mango Salad

1 cup of salad greens

1 mango

10 lychees

1 long red chilli

1 cup of fresh coriander

½ cup sliced spring onion

1 tablespoon olive oil

Salt and pepper to taste

DIRECTIONS

Peel the prawns leaving the tails on and carefully thread them onto skewers. In a bowl, mix together the garlic, honey, coconut aminos, chilli and lime juice. Marinate the prawn skewers in the mixture for 15 minutes. Heat a large pan over a medium heat on the stove with the coconut oil. Place the prawn skewers in the pan and cook each side for 2 minutes.

Serve the skewers with the Mango and Lychee salad.

Lychee & Mango Salad

Peel the lychees and cut them in half removing the seed. Peel the mango and slice the flesh away from the seed. Dice the flesh. Finely slice the red chilli and roughly chop the coriander. Place all of the ingredients in a large salad bowl and toss together for a fresh summery salad.

SERVES 4

Who said that you need a bread bun to enjoy an amazing fresh burger? These are the best burgers that you will ever have. They are so good that you won't even miss the processed bread bun! My family loves this meal because they can assemble their own burgers at the dinner table and customise them to their tastes.

chilli beef burgers

WITH FRESH BEETROOT

INGREDIENTS

- 500 grams of minced beef
- 1 onion
- 2 cloves garlic
- ½ teaspoon fresh ginger
- 1 handful of fresh coriander
- ½ long red chilli
- 1 egg
- ½ teaspoon of sea salt
- 1 tablespoon olive oil
- 1 beetroot, grated
- 1 tomato, sliced
- 4 lettuce leaves
- 1 avocado, sliced
- ¼ teaspoon sea salt

Sweet Potato Chips

- 4 large sweet potatoes
- 1 tablespoon melted coconut oil
- ½ teaspoon sea salt
- 1 sprig of rosemary

DIRECTIONS

To make the beef patties, finely chop the onion, ginger, garlic and chilli. Chop the coriander. Place all those ingredients in a large bowl along with the beef, egg and salt. With a fork or your hands, combine all the ingredients, then form 4 large meat patties. Heat the olive oil in a large pan over a medium heat. Place the meat patties down and cook for 5 minutes on each side.

While the patties are cooking, peel and grate the beetroot, slice the tomato, slice the avocado and wash the lettuce. Once the burgers are cooked assemble the burgers on a plate by stacking the ingredients. You can fasten them with a skewer if need be.

Sweet Potato Chips

Turn the oven on to 180 degrees and line a baking tray with baking paper. Peel the sweet potato and cut into 5mm slices lengthwise. Cut the slices into fries. Place the sweet potato on the baking tray in a single layer and toss with melted coconut oil. Sprinkle the sea salt and rosemary over the fries. Place in the oven and bake for 8 minutes, turn and then bake another 8 minutes or until golden brown.

Cooking time may vary depending on how thick you have cut your chips.

SERVES 4

pork & coconut meatballs

IN HOMEMADE TOMATO SAUCE

INGREDIENTS

500 grams of pork mince

½ cup of shredded coconut

1 cup coriander, chopped

1 onion, diced

1 garlic clove, crushed

1 tablespoon coconut oil

Salt to taste

Sauce

1 onion, diced

1 garlic clove, crushed

1 teaspoon fresh ginger, crushed

1 tablespoon olive oil

8 ripe tomatoes or 2 x 400ml cans of tomatoes

2 tablespoons of tomato paste

1 tablespoon coconut aminos

½ teaspoon chilli powder

½ teaspoon sea salt

½ cup water

DIRECTIONS

To start, make the sauce. Dice the onion, garlic and ginger. Heat the olive oil in a pan over a medium heat on the stove. Sauté the onion, garlic and ginger until the onion is transparent. Add the tomatoes, tomato paste, water, coconut aminos, salt and chilli. Let simmer for 15 minutes, stirring every 5 minutes. While the sauce is simmering you can start making the meatballs.

Dice the onion and garlic. In a large bowl, add the pork mince, garlic, onion, shredded coconut, coriander and salt. Mix together with your hands or a fork. Use a teaspoon to form small meatballs. Heat a large pan over a medium heat with the coconut oil. Place the meatballs in the pan and brown each side, rolling them gently in the pan. Repeat until all of the meatballs are cooked.

Once all of the meatballs are cooked, pour the sauce all around the meatballs and garnish with fresh herbs.

SERVES 4–6

This is such a great dish for the little ones and adults alike. The chicken has a yummy, crunchy golden brown texture that can't be beaten. My kids will eat anything if it is on a skewer. My daughter, Mackenzie, who is four years old, calls these skewers "lollypop chicken" so that is where we got the name from.

coconut lollypop chicken

INGREDIENTS

2 large chicken breasts

½ cup coconut flour

Salt and pepper to taste

3 eggs

1 tablespoon coconut oil

Smashed Lime Avocado

1 large ripe avocado

1 lime, juiced

Salt and pepper to taste

To make this dish more adult you can add your favourite spices to the coconut flour such as paprika, chilli, mixed herbs or lemon pepper.

Get creative!

Tip...

DIRECTIONS

Slice each chicken breast lengthwise into 5 or 6 pieces. Thread the chicken onto skewers. You should be able to make about 10 skewers.

Lightly beat the eggs together in a wide shallow bowl until combined. Mix the coconut flour with the salt and pepper and place the coconut flour mix on a flat plate. Roll the chicken sticks in the coconut flour. Then roll the skewers in the egg mixture. Lastly, roll them again in the coconut flour for a second coat. Heat a large pan over a medium heat with the coconut oil. Place 4 chicken skewers in the pan and turn over when golden brown. Repeat on the other side and cook completely through. Place in a warm oven while you cook the rest of the chicken skewers.

Serve with sweet potato rounds and smashed lime avocado.

SERVES 4

Smashed Lime Avocado

Cut the avocado in half, remove the stone and scoop out the flesh and place on a large chopping board. Sprinkle with the salt and pepper and squeeze the juice of 1 lime. With a fork roughly smash the avocado on the board. Serve on top of meats, fish or as a side to the coconut lollypop chicken.

"LIFE IS UNCERTAIN.
EAT DESSERT FIRST."
Ernestine Ulmer

treats AND sweets

Just because I don't eat refined sugar does not mean that I can't enjoy desserts and treats. In fact, I enjoy my desserts and treats more than I ever did in the past because I don't feel guilty about eating them. I know that I will wake up feeling good the next day and not sluggish. There is an amazing array of beautiful treats made from real food ingredients that can be enjoyed and here I have put a few together for you to try out.

red velvet brownies

INGREDIENTS

200 grams of raw beetroot

½ cup melted coconut oil

½ cup honey

2 large eggs

½ cup raw cacao powder

1 teaspoon baking soda

2 tablespoons coconut flour

Pinch of salt

Sugar Free Chocolate Frosting

10 medjool dates, pitted

2 tablespoons of raw cacao powder

2 tablespoons of coconut oil

1 teaspoon vanilla extract

1 pinch of salt

DIRECTIONS

Preheat the oven to 180 degrees and line a 28cm x 18cm baking dish with baking paper. Peel the beetroot and cut into 4–6 pieces. Place in the food processor and finely chop, or you can grate with a box grater. Add the coconut oil, honey, eggs and salt; combine the ingredients. Add the cacao, bi-carb soda and coconut flour; mix until combined. Pour the mixture into the baking dish and place in the oven for 25 minutes or until a skewer comes out clean. Let the brownie cool and cut into bite size squares, or use a round cookie cutter to make round brownies and top with chocolate frosting and raspberries for something a bit more fancy.

MAKES 8 LARGE OR 20 BITE SIZE SERVINGS

Sugar Free Chocolate Frosting

Cover the dates with hot water for 10 minutes to soften them. Drain the water then place the dates, cacao, coconut oil, vanilla and salt into the food processor and blitz. You will have to stop the processor and scrape down the sides several times. Continue to process until you have the consistency of frosting. This may take some time depending on your food processor.

intage Cafe

bliss balls

TRIPLE CHOCOLATE

INGREDIENTS

- 1 cup dried dates
- 1 cup almonds
- 2 tablespoons of raw cacao powder
- 1 cup desiccated coconut
- ½ cup cacao nibs
- 2 teaspoons honey
- 1 tablespoon raw cacao powder to coat

DIRECTIONS

Place all the ingredients except the cacao nibs in the food processor and blitz until it becomes doughy. This may take a while depending on the power of your food processor. Place the cacao nibs in the food processor and gently mix into the dough, but not chopped too finely. With a teaspoon, roll the mixture into balls. Coat with raw cacao powder by sifting the powder over the balls and rolling them in the powder. Place in the fridge to set for 1 hour.

MAKES 18

GINGER & CASHEW

INGREDIENTS

- 1 cup dried dates
- 1 cup cashew nuts
- 1 ½ teaspoons of ground ginger
- ½ teaspoon of cinnamon
- 2 teaspoons honey
- ¼ cup extra cashew nuts
- ¼ cup of sesame seeds to coat

DIRECTIONS

Place the dates, 1 cup of cashew nuts, ginger, cinnamon and honey in the food processor and blitz until it becomes doughy. This may take a while depending on the power of your food processor. Place the extra cashews in the food processor and gently mix into the dough, but do not chop them too finely. With a teaspoon roll the mixture into balls. Coat with sesame seeds by rolling the balls in the seeds. Place in the fridge to set for 1 hour.

MAKES 18

TANGY LIME & COCONUT

INGREDIENTS

- 1 cup dried dates
- 1 cup almonds
- Juice & zest of 1 lime
- 2 cups shredded coconut
- ¼ cup desiccated coconut

DIRECTIONS

Place dates, almonds and 1 ½ cups of shredded coconut in the food processor and blitz until finely processed. Add the lime zest and juice; process further until the mixture becomes doughy. With a teaspoon, roll the mixture into balls. Mix ½ cup of shredded coconut and ¼ cup of desiccated coconut together. Coat the rolled balls in the coconut by rolling the balls in the coconut and pressing gently. Place in the fridge to set for 1 hour.

MAKES 18

I really love these little cakes. Before committing to real food I had never really made or tried raw recipes like this before. One of my favourite local cafés makes a few lovely raw treats and this cake is inspired by my visits there. I personally think that this cake is healthy enough to eat any time of the day, even for breakfast.

MINI RAW carrot cakes WITH CASHEW CREAM

INGREDIENTS

3 cups of grated carrot

1 cup raw walnuts

1 cup pitted dates

½ cup shredded coconut

1 tablespoon of honey

1 tablespoon coconut oil

½ teaspoon cinnamon

½ teaspoon nutmeg

½ teaspoon ground ginger

¼ teaspoon of sea salt

Pistachio nuts and extra cinnamon to garnish

Cashew Cream

1 cup raw cashews, soaked min 3 hours

¼ cup water

3 tablespoons of honey

⅓ cup coconut oil, melted

1 teaspoon of vanilla extract

½ lemon, juiced

¼ teaspoon sea salt

DIRECTIONS

Peel and grate the carrots and set aside. In a food processor, place the dates and walnuts. Process roughly, keeping the mixture chunky. Transfer to a large bowl; add the coconut, spices, honey, coconut oil and salt, and combine. Add the carrot and mix until well combined. Scoop the cake mix into a greased muffin pan, firmly pressing the mixture into each pan. Place in the fridge for 3 hours to allow to set before removing the cakes from the pans.

Once they are set, lay on a plate and top with cashew cream frosting and garnish with the pistachio nuts. Place back in the fridge to set.

Cashew Cream

Soak cashews for a minimum of 3 hours but overnight is preferable. Drain and rinse soaked cashews in clean water. In a food processor or blender, process the cashews until they make very smooth nut butter. Add the water, honey, vanilla, salt and lemon juice. Blend until very smooth, scraping down the sides as needed. Add melted coconut oil and blend until combined and very smooth.

Serve on top of carrot cakes, pancakes or use as a sweet dipping sauce.

SERVES 6

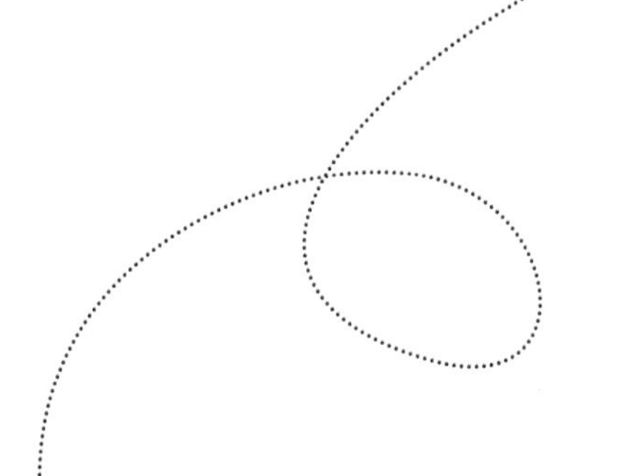

These strawberry and almond bars are the perfect treat that the whole family will enjoy. Once you know how to make the base you can get creative with your own toppings. I sometimes make the base and store it in the fridge just in case I need a healthy dessert in a hurry, it will keep for a few weeks.

strawberry & almond BARS

INGREDIENTS

Base

- 1 cup dried dates
- 1 cup almonds
- 2 tablespoons of cacao
- ½ tablespoon of coconut oil
- ¼ cup sliced almonds

Topping

- 2 cups of strawberries (fresh or frozen)
- 1 tablespoon of honey
- ½ teaspoon of cinnamon
- ½ teaspoon of vanilla extract
- 1 tablespoon coconut oil
- 1 cup fresh strawberries, sliced

DIRECTIONS

Base

In a food processor, place the dates, almonds and cacao. Process until fine and crumbly. Add the coconut oil and process further until combined. Add the sliced almonds and mix through. Line a baking tin or dish with parchment paper and press the mixture into the base of the tin. Place in fridge to set while making the topping.

Topping

In a saucepan over a medium heat, place the coconut oil and melt. Cut the strawberries in half and add to the saucepan along with the honey, vanilla and cinnamon. Let simmer over a low heat for 5 minutes until the mixture looks gooey.

Remove from the heat and let cool. Assemble this dish right before serving by placing the base on a large serving plate, top with the cooled strawberry coulis, and then top with the fresh sliced strawberries. Cut into bars and serve immediately.

MAKES 12 PIECES

You had me at lemon! I love lemon desserts and this dish is no exception despite it's healthy ingredients. This dessert is so easy to make, and it really does taste very indulgent.

lemon & coconut tart

INGREDIENTS

For the Crust

- 3 tablespoons coconut oil
- 1 tablespoon honey
- 2 cups unsweetened shredded coconut
- 1 cup almond flour
- 1 pinch sea salt
- 2 egg whites (save the yolks for the lemon filling)

Filling

- 3 eggs + 2 egg yolks
- 5 tablespoons maple syrup
- ⅓ cup lemon juice
- Zest of 1 lemon
- ¼ cup coconut flour

DIRECTIONS

Preheat the oven to 180 degrees celsius and line the base of a 22cm pie or baking dish with baking paper. Melt the coconut oil in a medium saucepan over medium heat. Add the honey, shredded coconut, almond flour and salt. Mix until well combined and remove from the heat. Add the egg whites and mix in until it becomes very sticky. Pat the mixture onto the bottom and up the sides of the prepared pan and press down firmly. Bake for 8–10 minutes or until slightly brown and then remove from the oven.

Meanwhile, start preparing the filling. In a large bowl, with an electric mixer or blender, beat together the eggs and egg yolks until frothy. Add the remaining ingredients and beat for two additional minutes. Pour the filling over the baked crust and bake for 20 minutes, or until the centre is set. Let it cool completely and serve.

SERVES 8

MINI CHEESECAKES

INGREDIENTS

Base

- 1 cup almonds
- ½ cup dates
- 2 tablespoons of coconut oil
- Pinch of sea salt

Filling

- 1 ½ cups raw cashew nuts (soaked for 3 hours)
- ¼ cup coconut milk
- ½ cup fresh lime juice
- 2 tablespoons of lime zest
- ½ cup pineapple, finely chopped
- 3 tablespoons of honey
- 6 tablespoons of coconut oil

DIRECTIONS

Put all of the base ingredients in the food processor and blitz until it is fine and sticky. Place 1 large tablespoon of the base mixture into the bottom of each muffin patty or mould and press down to line the bottom of each pan. You should be able to make 8 bases. Place the bases in the freezer to set while you make the topping.

To make the topping, drain the cashews and place in the food processor and process until you make smooth cashew butter. Add all of the other ingredients except the pineapple and blitz for a further minute or until very smooth. Add the chopped pineapple and stir into the mixture, keeping the pineapple slightly chunky. Remove the bases from the freezer, spoon the topping onto the bases, put back in the freezer to set for a minimum of 1 hour.

About 15 minutes before you are ready to serve the desserts take them out of the freezer to let thaw a little. Place the desserts on a plate and serve. Top with freshly diced pineapple and lime zest.

SERVES 8

Tip...

Instead of making individual servings, you could make one large cheesecake by using a cake tin.

roasted nuts

INDIAN SPICED ALMONDS

INGREDIENTS

2 cups of raw almonds

1 tablespoon of olive oil

½ teaspoon ground ginger

½ teaspoon of ground cumin

½ teaspoon of ground paprika

½ teaspoon of ground chilli

Pinch of sea salt

DIRECTIONS

Preheat the oven to 150 degrees celsius and prepare a baking tray by lining it with baking paper. Place all the ingredients in a large bowl and mix until the nuts are completely coated. Lay out the mixed nuts on the baking tray in a single layer and place in the oven for 10 minutes, stir to turn them after 5 minutes. Serve straight away or store in an air-tight jar.

MAPLE & ROSEMARY ROASTED MIXED NUTS

INGREDIENTS

½ cup raw pecan nuts

½ cup raw cashew nuts

½ cup raw brazil nuts

½ cup raw almonds

2 tablespoons natural maple syrup

1 sprig of fresh rosemary (chopped)

Pinch of sea salt

DIRECTIONS

Preheat the oven to 150 degrees celsius and prepared a baking tray by lining it with baking paper. Place all the ingredients in a large bowl and mix until the nuts are completely coated. Lay out the mixed nuts on the baking tray in a single layer and place in the oven for 10 minutes, stir to turn them after 5 minutes. Serve straight away or store in an air-tight jar.

CHILLI LIME MACADAMIAS

INGREDIENTS

2 cups of raw macadamia nuts

1 tablespoon of olive oil

1 teaspoon ground chilli

½ teaspoon ground paprika

1 lime, juiced

Pinch of sea salt

DIRECTIONS

Preheat the oven to 150 degrees celsius and prepare a baking tray by lining it with baking paper. Place all the ingredients in a large bowl and mix until the nuts are completely coated. Lay out the mixed nuts on the baking tray in a single layer and place in the oven for 10 minutes, stir to turn them after 5 minutes. Serve straight away or store in an air-tight jar.

coconutty fruity drinks

PINEAPPLE, COCONUT & MINT

INGREDIENTS

1 cup of fresh pineapple

1 handful fresh mint leaves

2 cups coconut water

DIRECTIONS

Place all ingredients in the food processor and blitz until smooth and combined. Serve with ice and garnish with fresh pineapple and mint.

WATERMELON & COCONUT

INGREDIENTS

1 cup frozen watermelon

2 cups coconut water

DIRECTIONS

Place all ingredients in the food processor and blitz until smooth and combined. Serve over ice in a fancy glass for a fresh summery drink.

KIWI, APPLE & COCONUT

INGREDIENTS

3 ripe kiwi fruit

1 cup fresh apple juice

1 cup coconut water

DIRECTIONS

Peel the kiwi fruit then place all ingredients in the food processor and blitz until smooth and combined. Serve over ice and garnish with fresh kiwi fruit.

"THE KITCHEN REALLY IS THE CASTLE ITSELF. THIS IS WHERE WE SPEND OUR HAPPIEST MOMENTS AND WHERE WE FIND THE JOY OF BEING A FAMILY."

Mario Batali

TOOLS FOR A REAL FOOD KITCHEN

the Real Food PANTRY

Below are the ingredients that are used throughout this book. This is not a comprehensive list but will help you to get on your way with your real food pledge.

In the cupboard

Nuts – macadamia nuts, almonds, cashew nuts, pecan nuts, pistachio nuts, brazil nuts, walnuts

Seeds – chia seeds, sunflower seeds, flaxseed (linseed), sesame seeds

Macadamia and almond pastes

Coconut cream

Coconut milk

Shredded coconut

Cacao powder

Cacao nibs

Dates – medjool and dried

Honey

Natural maple syrup

Apple cider vinegar

Dried spices and herbs

Salt

Coconut flour

Tinned tomatoes

Tinned fish

Herbal tea – ginger, licorice, peach, lemon, chamomile

Olive Oil

Coconut Oil

In the fridge

Coconut aminos – buy from your local health food store

Fish sauce

Mustard

Coconut yoghurt

Coconut water

Fresh almond milk (home-made is best)

Sliced ready to eat meats

Eggs

Sliced salmon

Avocado

Fish

Seafood

Olives in olive oil

Meats

In the freezer

Frozen berries

Frozen mango

Pureed pumpkin

Frozen vegetables

Prawns

Frozen bananas

From the farmer's market

Capsicum

Cauliflower

Green beans

Broccoli

Fennel

Lettuce

Mixed salad greens

Sweet potato

Asparagus

Zucchini

Pumpkin

Beetroot

Carrots

Ginger

Onions

Garlic

Bok Choy

Celery

Radish

Basil

Coriander

Rosemary

Dill

Parsley

Lemon Grass

Kaffir lime leaves

Fruit & berries

Apples

Oranges

Kiwi fruit

Mandarins

Lemons

Limes

Grapefruit

Strawberries

Blueberries

Raspberries

Mango

Bananas

Peaches

Apricots

Grapes

Melons

Conversion CHART

I'm aware that cooking measurements and ingredient names are not the same in various countries of the world. My secret squirrel recipe testers made me aware of all of the differences which has helped me with this conversion chart. In Australia we use metric measurements but we also measure a lot of our ingredients by the cupful. In Australia our cup is approximately 250ml. I have converted the measurements from this book and also given you the different names of ingredients for your ease.

Weight Measurements

Australian weights	Equivalent U.S. weights
30 gm	1 ounce
50-60 gm	2 ounces
90-100gm	3 ounces
125 gm	4 ounces
225gm	6 ounces
250 gm	8 ounces
500 gm	16 ounces
1 kg	2 1/4 pounds
2 kg	4 1/2 pounds

Liquid Measurements

Australian liquid measurements	Equivalent US measurements
1 ml	1/4 teaspoon
2 ml	1/2 teaspoon
5 ml	1 teaspoon
15 ml	1 tablespoon
60 ml	1/4 cup
80 ml	1/3 cup
125 ml	1/2 cup
170 ml	2/3 cup
190 ml	3/4 cup
250 ml	1 cup
500 ml	2 cups
1 litre	1 quart

Oven Temperatures

Equivalent in Celsius	Equivalent in Fahrenheit
120	250
150	300
160–180	325–350
190–200	375–400
220–230	425–450
250–260	475–500
270–290	525–550

Ingredient Conversions

Beef mince	Ground beef
Beetroot	Beets
Capsicum	Bell pepper
Cos lettuce	Romaine lettuce
Coriander	Cilantro
Prawn	Shrimp
Sultanas	Raisin

resources & READING

These are some of the books that I have read and enjoyed. When my friends ask me to recommend a book, these are the ones that I tell them to read.

IT STARTS WITH FOOD
Melissa & Dallas Hartwig

SALT SUGAR FAT, HOW THE FOOD GIANTS HOOKED US
Michael Moss

SWEET POISON
David Gillespie

PRIMAL BODY PRIMAL MIND
Nora Gedgaudas

PALEO SOLUTION
Robb Wolf

IN DEFENCE OF FOOD
Michael Pollan

WHEAT BELLY
William Davis

THE PRIMAL BLUE PRINT
Mark Sisson

THANK YOU, *Thank You* THANK YOU!

Making this lifestyle and recipe book started as a fun little project. I initially thought that I wanted to create an e-book for my blog Real Food Pledge. As I wrote and created the book, I dreamed bigger. The book became larger than life, it then went from an e-book to an amazing print book. As I went along I thought that if it was going to be a print book I had to create something inspiring that was fun, with beautiful pictures, helpful information and amazing recipes. I could not have achieved this amazingness on my own; I needed a team of supportive and talented people.

I am so grateful for all the support and encouragement that I have had from my family, friends and the girls in my office. My Mum, Gran, Rachel, Angelique, Toni-Lee, Jill, Therese and Warwick, thank you for all the, support, proof reading, brain storming and workshopping that you have all done along the way.

Thank you to all the people that follow me on Facebook, Instagram and my blog, Real Food Pledge. You are all wonderful and inspire me – I love connecting with you and talking about our shared passion… real food.

To Jo Anderson who eagerly came on board to help me with the photography and food styling; what an amazing talent. Jo shared my vision for the photography and pulled it all together. I cooked, she styled and took amazing photos and then we ate! Jo made the images look better than I could have imagined and went the extra mile. It was lots of fun.

To my secret squirrel recipe testers, there are too many to name, but you were all wonderful and I really enjoyed connecting with you all. It is wonderful how food can bring perfect strangers together from all over the world. Your feedback was invaluable and your input helped me to tweak the recipes to perfection.

I had beautiful recipes that I loved, outstanding photos and perfected text, but I needed it to all come together. That's when Simone and the team from Shac Communications stepped in and brought it all together with the amazing design work. Thank you for taking this project on and having the vision to bring it together ready for publishing. I am forever grateful.

Thank you to my husband Cameron and my kids, Levi, Riley and Mackenzie for being my number one guinea pigs and trying all the recipes that I create. Boys, I love that you think that the cauliflower mash is potato and that the pumpkin pancakes are yummy, even though you would never knowingly eat pumpkin. Kenzie, you are a super cute girl and the perfect smiling prop for my book. It was so much fun when you were so excited to come to a picnic with mummy, that you came straight from kindy with aboriginal face paint all over you! And finally a BIG thank you to Cameron for giving me the space to embark on such a huge project and having the patience to wait for me to take photos of our food before we eat. I love you lots.

Lastly, thank you to you for buying a copy of this book. I hope you enjoy it as much as I enjoyed creating it.

Caralee xxx

GET CONNECTED

VISIT MY BLOG

www.realfoodpledge.com

❧

TWEET ME

@caraleecaldwell

❧

FOLLOW ME ON INSTAGRAM FOR DAILY EATS
OR SEND ME YOUR REAL FOOD CREATIONS:

@realfoodpledge

❧

FOLLOW ME ON PINTEREST FOR
REAL FOOD INSPIRATION:

Real Food Pledge

❧

FIND ME ON FACEBOOK FOR DAILY REAL FOOD UPDATES:

www.facebook/realfoodpledge

INDEX